This Book belongs to

....

Melissa
Forti's
Christmas
Baking
Book

Photographs by
Danny Bernardini

To Miss P.
The purest love I have ever known.
I will never forget you.
And to my beloved Rudy,
who is my guardian and furry child.
No love was greater than the one we three shared.

Melissa Forti's Christmas Baking Book

Prestel

Munich · London · New York

My first meeting with Melissa was unforgettable. For the German TV series Kitchen Impossible, my friend, Tim Mälzer, sent me to Melissa's Tea Room in Sarzana. My task was to recreate Melissa's tiramisu cake, but as many people know, baking and cooking are not the same thing. I failed dramatically at the task.

Failure, however, is one of life's greatest challenges, but for me it does not mean a tragic end. Instead, it signals the end of a learning process, albeit a tough one. By failing, you learn that something does NOT work. What results is the discovery of a new approach—a new way of tackling things—which brings us to Melissa's work.

When you get to know Melissa personally, you immediately sense her perceptiveness and keen style. The fire in her eyes and the intensity of her words enrich everything that she bakes. The cakes and gateaux themselves are reminiscent of their creator's graceful silhouette. They are brimming with authenticity and good taste. Every ingredient makes its presence felt and expertly interacts with the others. It is as if every cake is infused with a kind of excitement.

Melissa's book is an invitation to try your hand at her creations. And that, as I know from experience, is impossible to do without the recipes. For this reason, I am delighted that we now have the opportunity to immerse ourselves in Melissa's world with detailed instructions to guide us. My advice to the reader is to keep strictly to the recipes; if you do, the results of your baking will be superb. For my part, I succeeded with my second tiramisu cake because I followed Melissa's step-by-step directions.

The cordiality and vivacity that sparkle in every Italian sentence that Melissa speaks can be tasted in each of her recipes. However, her Christmas creations are exceptional, providing an extra helping of warmth and comfort, ensuring that this season of togetherness is a sensual feast for the heart.

Tim Raue

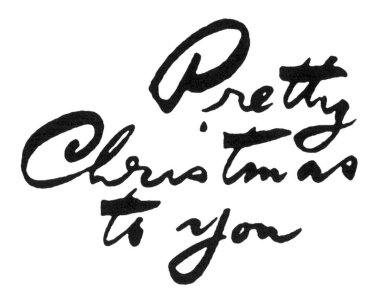

Pretty Christmas to you

I am sitting at my desk, in front of my computer, on a stormy Italian winter morning.

Today, my two cats are enjoying sitting by my side; it's cold and rainy outside, and they love to snuggle in search of a warm spot.

I am enjoying a slice of cake and a hot cup of coffee, of course.

My breakfast is usually sweet. And sweet is also this time of the year… Christmas is coming!

When I was offered the chance to write a book about Christmas baking, I was overwhelmed with excitement! There isn't a better time of the year to turn on the oven and to bake like there is no tomorrow! And so, I quickly started dusting off my personal baking notebook, where I write all my recipes for the festive season, and I was ready to ramble on happily about ingredients like: citrus zests, winter berries, cinnamon sticks, liquors etc. I stopped for a moment and realized that I didn't want to simply write a book about Christmas recipes. For that, we have the Internet, and I am sure you all have your fair share of amazing recipes, too. As I go through life, I find myself in search of deeper meanings. This is why, before sharing my recipes with you, I wish to stop for a moment to think about what Christmas means to me and perhaps to some of you, too.

In Italian, the holiday is called "Natale," which means "birth." Whether or not you look at Christmas from a religious point of view, Christmas is also a time for gatherings to celebrate life, family, friends, the past, the present, and the future. In a sense, we are all united, with the same purpose: to share time together and to reset whatever we feel needs resetting. It's like time stands still for a moment; we pause, we gather together, we share, and we hope for new beginnings. From north to south, from east to west, we cook and we bake following old traditions and creating new ones.

As you probably know by now, I am on a quest to tackle the world's great pastry heritage, as well as reinventing recipes while exploring new territories.

This is the fun part of my job. I present to you some of the greatest holiday recipes I have baked, created, and tasted throughout my personal life journey. From all-time favorite classics to recipes you might read for the first time.

I wish to pay my most humble and respectful honors to the vast Italian bakery tradition, as well as presenting my take on international recipes so you can bake for those you love, exploring the history and traditions of other countries and perhaps to tell stories about them. At least at Christmas, we may feel as if we were all sitting at "the same table," where there is only one thing that matters: being together.

Buon Natale!

With love,

Melissa

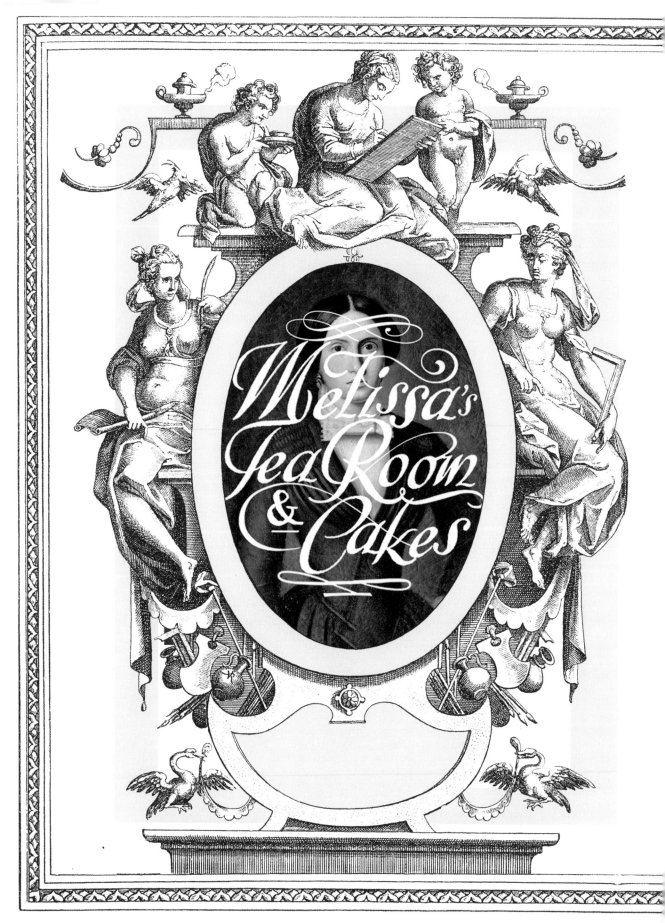

Large Cakes & Showstoppers

Small Treats, Other Bakes & More

Christmas Breads & Other Pastries

LARGE CAKES
& Showstoppers

Galette des Rois

Ingredients

About 6 servings

For the pastry cream
- 3 large egg yolks
- *½ cup* plus *1 tablespoon (110g)* sugar
- *¼ cup (30g)* organic cornstarch
- *1 tablespoon (15ml)* freshly-squeezed organic lemon juice
- *1 ½ cups (350ml)* whole milk
- *1 teaspoon* vanilla bean paste or pure vanilla extract

For the frangipane cream
- *½ cup (115g)* or *1 stick* unsalted butter
- *⅜ cup* plus *1 tablespoon (75g)* sugar
- *2 medium* organic eggs, at room temperature
- *1 teaspoon* vanilla bean paste or pure vanilla extract
- *1 teaspoon* orange blossom water
- Freshly-grated zest of *1* organic lemon
- *1 cup* plus *1 tablespoon (100g)* almond flour
- *1 tablespoon* plus *1 teaspoon (20g)* all-purpose flour

For the egg wash
- *2* organic eggs
- *1 medium* egg yolk
- *1 tablespoon* plus *1 teaspoon (20ml)* whole milk
- Pinch of salt

For the cake
- *2 rectangular* sheets frozen puff pastry, cold

For the sugar syrup
- *¾ cup (150g)* sugar

*P*repared in France to celebrate the Epiphany, Galette des Rois is one of those pretty creations that magically bring people together. Traditionally, in poor families, la fève—a broad bean—was hidden in the filling, while the wealthy used a little king figurine. And whoever found the prize was declared "king of the day." Customs like these make Christmas a truly wonderful time of the year!

Note: The holidays are a very busy time of year, so I advise you to use frozen puff pastry for this recipe, providing it is of the best quality. Galette des Rois is already a little time consuming and you deserve to enjoy this wonderful preparation with your family and friends, I would rather you have fun decorating it instead of going crazy making puff pastry. Of course, if you wish to make it from scratch, please feel free to do so.

Method

Make the pastry cream in a medium-sized bowl by combining the egg yolks, sugar, cornstarch, and lemon juice. Then whisk until pale.

In a medium-sized saucepan, bring the milk to a gentle boil. Pour a small amount into the egg yolk mixture and stir quickly to temper the eggs. Pour the tempered egg mixture into the saucepan, place over low heat and cook, stirring until thick. Add the vanilla. Strain through a sieve into a large-sized bowl, then cover with plastic wrap and refrigerate until ready to use.

Make the frangipane cream in the bowl of a stand mixer fitted with the paddle attachment. Beat together the butter and sugar on low until just combined. Add the eggs, vanilla, orange blossom water, and lemon zest and beat until just combined. Add the almond flour and all-purpose flour and beat until creamy. Gradually fold in the pastry cream—the mixture should be creamy but a little stiff, so you may not need to add all of the pastry cream. Any leftover pastry cream can be refrigerated for a couple of days or served with fresh fruit. Refrigerate the frangipane for about 1 hour or until set. Transfer to a piping bag fitted with a medium round tip and refrigerate until ready to use.

→

Make the egg wash in a small bowl by whisking together the egg, egg yolk, milk, and salt. Strain into a small bowl.

To make the cake, keep your hands and the puff pastry cold. Fill a bowl with ice water and set it near your work area in case you need to chill your hands.

Place 1 sheet of puff pastry on a piece of parchment paper set on a work surface. Arrange an 8-inch (20-cm) ring or round cake pan on the parchment paper and use a sharp knife to cut around it and cut out the first round of puff pastry. Refrig-

erate and repeat with the other sheet of puff pastry and an 8 ½-inch (22-cm) ring or second round cake pan. Brush the egg wash around the edges of both puff pastry rounds, making sure not to drip it over the sides onto the parchment paper, or the Galette des Rois will not rise.

Pipe the frangipane cream on the first puff pastry round, starting from the center. Create three circles slightly overlapping each other, working your way towards the sides, leaving a margin of about 0.05 inches (1.5 cm) all the way around. At this point, the fève can be hidden. Remove

the second round of puff pastry from the refrigerator and place it on top of the first. Seal the edges by pressing down on them with a fork. Refrigerate for at least 1 hour before decorating.

Make the sugar syrup in a small saucepan by combining the sugar and ⅔ cup (150ml) water and cook over medium heat until the sugar is fully dissolved. Refrigerate until ready to use. Preheat the oven to 400°F (200°C).

Using a craft knife or any very sharp blade, score 2 curved lines about ¾ inch (2 mm) deep into the top of the cake, starting from the center and moving toward the edges. With a round, medium-sized piping tip, create a hole in the center to help release steam during baking. Brush the top of the cake with the remaining egg wash and bake for 8 to 10 minutes, then lower the oven temperature to 325°F (160°C) and bake for 30 to 35 minutes. Brush the cake with the sugar syrup and let cool before serving.

Christmas Pavlova

(AND THE MANY STORIES SURROUNDING IT)

*H*ow can a simple recipe like this one cause so much stir in the pastry world? Historians have spent years tracking down the origins of this cake. As many of you know, Australians and New Zealanders are, to this day, the proud "owners" of the recipe, but history isn't totally clear on the matter. German immigrants brought Schaumtorte, a meringue-based dessert, to America, and while a close cousin, it wasn't quite the Pavlova we know today—it's not a secret that Germans created some of the best cakes in the world!

Another possibility is that meringue-based cakes became popular in many households when the first electric beaters became available for sale in 1900. Finally, egg whites could be whipped in a matter of minutes, which led to Pavlova becoming the go-to cake at any stylish tea party. But the story I love most is the one about a chef in New Zealand who fell in love with the beauty of a Russian ballerina named Anna Matveyevna Pavlova, and created this light-as-a-feather cake to celebrate her grace and charm.

Whatever the origins of Pavlova, it is delicious any time of the year and at Christmas, it is particularly stunning as a centerpiece. You can play with different shapes and sizes, and decorate it as you wish. If you make a larger or smaller Pavlova , you may need to adjust the baking time. Your guests and family will be stunned by how gorgeous it looks!

Ingredients

About 6/8 servings

- 4 large organic egg whites, at room temperature
- 1 cup (200g) granulated sugar
- 1 teaspoon freshly-squeezed organic lemon juice
- 1 tablespoon organic cornstarch
- 1 teaspoon vanilla bean paste or pure vanilla extract

For the mascarpone cream
- 1 cup (240ml) heavy whipping cream
- Freshly-squeezed juice of 1 medium organic orange
- 9 ounces (225g) mascarpone cheese, at room temperature
- 1 cup (100g) confectioners' sugar
- ½ teaspoon orange oil or extract (optional)

To decorate
- ½ cup (50g) fresh cranberries
- ½ cup (50g) pomegranate arils
- Fresh rosemary sprigs

Method

Preheat the oven to 250°F (120°C) and line a baking sheet with parchment paper. Using an 8-inch (20-cm) round cake pan or ring mold, draw a circle on the parchment paper, then flip the parchment upside down to avoid contact with the Pavlova later.

In the bowl of a stand mixer fitted with the whisk attachment, whip the egg whites until frothy. Slowly add the sugar and whip until stiff peaks have formed. Add the lemon juice and cornstarch and whip until very stiff. Using the circle as a guide, gently spread the meringue into an 8-inch (20-cm) circle on the parchment, being careful not to deflate it. Using a small offset spatula, shape the meringue into a dome, staying within the circle you traced. Start swiping upwards to create the pattern in the photo, then press gently in the center to create an indentation. If there is any remaining meringue, use a pastry bag fitted with a small round piping tip to pipe little meringue drops onto the parchment. Bake for 1 ½ hours or until fully baked, light in weight, and dry. Let it cool completely on the baking sheet.

Make the mascarpone cream in the bowl of a stand mixer fitted with the whisk attachment, by whipping the heavy cream until medium-stiff peaks have formed. Then slowly add the orange juice and continue beating until fully stiff peaks have formed. Switch to the paddle attachment.

In a medium-sized bowl, use a rubber spatula or wooden spoon to stir the mascarpone until creamy and smooth. With the mixer on low, in small batches add the mascarpone to the cream mixture and then beat until fully incorporated. Add the confectioners' sugar and orange oil (optional).

Fill the center of the Pavlova with the mascarpone cream and decorate with fresh cranberries, pomegranate arils, rosemary sprigs, or whatever you like best.

Zuccotto Fiorentino

Ingredients

8 servings

For the sponge cake
- *6* large organic eggs, at room temperature
- *1 cup* plus *2 tablespoons (225g)* granulated sugar
- *1 ¾ cups (230g)* all-purpose flour
- Pinch of salt
- *1 teaspoon* vanilla bean paste or pure vanilla extract

For the ricotta cream filling
- *18 ounces (450g)* cow's milk ricotta cheese
- *Scant 1/3 cup (60g)* granulated sugar
- *½ cup (120ml)* heavy cream
- *1 tablespoon* unsweetened cocoa powder
- *2 ounces (50g)* small chocolate chips
- *1 ¾ ounces (45g)* candied orange peel, cut into small cubes

To decorate
- *3 tablespoons* unsweetened cocoa powder
- *1 cup* plus *2 teaspoons (250ml)* spiced liqueur, such as Alchermes

*A*hhhh! Once more, and probably for-ever, we have the Medici family to thank for this recipe. And more specifically, the amazing Catherine de' Medici, Queen consort of France, for whom this reci-pe was created. I remember, when I was young, my mother used to buy "Zuccotto" to bring as a gift when invited to holiday dinner parties. So, to me, it symbolizes celebration. It's also delicious!

Method

Preheat the oven to 350°F (180°C) and line the bottom of a 9 ½-inch (24-cm) round cake pan with parchment paper.

Make the sponge cake in the bowl of a stand mixer fitted with the whisk attach-ment. Whip the eggs and granulated sugar on medium-high for at least 15 to 20 min-utes, or until tripled in volume. Sift the flour twice, then very gently fold it into the egg mixture, making sure not to deflate the batter. Gently fold in the salt and vanilla. Pour into the parchment-lined pan and bake, without opening the oven door for 40 to 45 minutes. Let cool completely on a wire rack, then wrap in plastic wrap and freeze for 1 hour.

Make the ricotta cream filling by pressing the ricotta through a sieve into a large bowl, then adding the granulated sugar and stir just until creamy and combined. Do not over-mix or the ricotta will turn to liquid.

In another large bowl, use a hand-held mixer to whip the cream until stiff peaks form, then gently fold into the ricotta mixture. Transfer about 8 ounces (200g) of the ricotta cream to a small bowl. Add the cocoa powder, chocolate chips, and candied orange peel to the larger amount of ricotta cream and stir to combine. Transfer both mixtures to piping bags and refrigerate until ready to use.

Line a half-hemisphere cake pan or round glass bowl, about 4 ¼ x 6 ¾-inches (11 x 17-cm), with plastic wrap.

Cut the sponge cake into ½-inch (1.25-cm) thick slices and arrange inside the pre-pared cake pan, pressing gently to make sure they properly adhere to the sides. Reserve the leftover slices for the base of the cake. Using a pastry brush, brush the sponge cake with the spiced liqueur.

Pipe the white ricotta cream inside the sponge cake layer, filling the cake pan to the top. Use a spoon to scoop a small hole in the middle. Pipe the cocoa ricot-ta cream into the hole and use an offset spatula to smooth the surface. Arrange the remaining slices of sponge cake on top to create the base of the cake, brush with the spiced liqueur, cover with plas-tic wrap, and refrigerate for at least 4 hours and preferably overnight. The cake can also be frozen until ready to use; defrost for 1 hour before serving.

Turn out the cake onto a serving plate and dust with cocoa powder. Garnish as you please, with berries or chocolate shavings, and enjoy!

Croquembouche, Italian-Style

Ingredients

Serves 10 people or more

For the pâte à choux
- *1 ½ cups* plus *1 tablespoon (375ml)* whole milk
- *1 ½ cups* plus *1 tablespoon (375ml)* water
- *1 ⅓ cups (300g)* unsalted butter
- *½ teaspoon* granulated sugar
- *½ teaspoon* salt
- *3 ⅝ cups (450g)* bread flour (alternatively, Manitoba flour)
- *15 medium* organic eggs *(about 765g total)*
- *Confectioners' sugar,* for dusting

For the caramel
- *½ cup (125ml)* water
- *5 cups (1 kg)* granulated sugar
- *½ cup (120 ml)* liquid glucose or light corn syrup

For the crème chantilly
- *4 cups (1 liter)* heavy whipping cream
- *1 ¼ cups* plus *1 tablespoon (140g)* confectioners' sugar
- *1 teaspoon* vanilla bean paste, or pure vanilla extract

Equipment to make the paper cone
- *1 medium-firm piece* of cardboard paper, roughly 12 x 24-inch (60 x 30-cm)
- *Scissors*
- *Tape*
- *Parchment paper*

*N*othing shouts "celebration" quite like a croquembouche. In Paris, I've seen some of the tallest croquembouche ever. For Parisian pastry chefs, creating the tallest tower of delicious caramel bignès (cream puffs) is a matter of honor and a testimony to their professional skills. Creating the perfect croquembouche can be overwhelming and definitely time consuming, but do not despair. The hard work will pay off; the results will be more than satisfying!

This is my version of the famous dessert, using Italian-style bignès. They are irregularly shaped because they're not baked using the craquelin. Although traditionally filled with chantilly cream, pastry cream, or whipped cream, caramel works with almost any flavor, so you can play with different ingredients to suit the occasion. Add a dash of brandy to your pastry cream, or go one step further, filling the bignès with orange-infused chocolate cream.

I love to place my croquembouche right in the center of the table and decorate it with sparkling stars for a "wow" effect. It pairs well with a glass of sweet Italian wine like Moscato or Vin Santo, or for a more festive feel, a glass of Champagne will heighten the celebratory experience. As many of you know, I am all about "less is more," but at this time of year, I happily invite you to go overboard! At Christmas, more is more!

Note: This recipe yields about 120 medium bignès, plus 24 small. You will need a medium-firm sheet of cardboard paper, roughly 12 x 24-inch (60 x 30-cm) to build your croquembouche. Depending on how big you wish to make your croquembouche, you may have leftovers. Unfilled bignès can be well wrapped and frozen for up to 1 month.

Method

Make the paper cone by rolling the cardboard into a cone shape. The bigger the cone, the more bignès you will need. If you follow the size I suggest, you should have enough bignès to cover the entire cone. Use the tape to secure the cone into position.

Using scissors, trim the base so the cone will sit flat on the counter. Trim the tip at the top to make it flat. Wrap 1 or 2 sheets of parchment paper around the cone so the bignès will stick to it. Cut a square of parchment and place it over the top, thereby closing the hole. The small square provides a "hat" or "cork," so that the cream puffs will not fall inside the cone. Finally, trim any excess parchment and you are ready to go!

Preheat the oven to 450°F (230°C) and line a baking sheet with parchment paper.

Make the pâte à choux in a medium-sized saucepan, by bringing the milk, butter, sugar, salt, and 1 ½ cups plus 1 tablespoon (375ml) of water to a boil. Remove from the heat, then use a wooden spoon to quickly stir in the flour. Place over low to medium heat and cook for about 1 minute, or until a film forms on the bottom of the pan and the back of the spoon. Transfer to the bowl of a stand mixer fitted with the paddle attachment and let cool slightly.

In a medium-sized bowl, quickly whisk the eggs. With the mixer on low, gradu-

→

ally add the eggs. When the eggs are fully incorporated, the dough should have a dense but creamy texture that is perfect for piping, and the bowl should feel warm, but not hot to the touch. Transfer to a pastry bag fitted with a medium round tip (I use an Ateco 806 tip, but you can use any round or star-shaped tip) and pipe medium-sized bignès (3-cm diameter) on a baking sheet (you will need to do this in several batches), leaving a little space between each so that they do not touch each other while baking. Dust with a little confectioners' sugar and bake for 5 minutes, then reduce the oven temperature to 350°F (180°C) and continue baking for 30 minutes or until golden. Let cool completely.

Make the crème Chantilly in a stand mixer fitted with a whisk attachment or by using a hand-held mixer. Whip the heavy whipping cream first on slow speed and then increase to high speed until medium-stiff peaks are formed. Add the confectioners' sugar and vanilla and whip until stiff, being careful not to whip it too much or the cream will curdle. Transfer to a pastry bag fitted with a small to me-

dium-sized piping tip and fill each bignè by inserting the piping tip into the bottom and squeezing the cream inside. Be gentle or the bignè might break from the pressure you apply while piping.

Before you make the caramel, fill a bowl with ice water and set it near your work area in case you burn your fingers on the caramel, which is extremely hot. In a large saucepan over medium heat, combine the sugar, glucose, and ½ cup (125ml) water and cook until golden amber in color. While heating the mixture, do not stir to avoid crystallization. You can either brush the sides of the pan using a wet pastry brush or gently swirl the pan around. Remove from the heat and carefully start dipping the bignès into the hot caramel and pressing them onto the paper cone, starting from the bottom and working up to the top.

Decorate as you please. Make your triumphant entrance, place your croquembouche in the center of your Christmas table, and wait for your guests to scream, "WHOOOOO!!!!"

Torta Di Datteri e Caramello

STICKY TOFFEE CAKE (BUT NOT REALLY)

Ingredients

About 10 servings

For the cake
- *12 ¼ ounces (350g)* pitted dates
- *4 ½ cups plus 1 tablespoon (550g)* all-purpose flour
- *5 teaspoons* baking powder
- *3 teaspoons* ground cinnamon
- *1 teaspoon* ground nutmeg
- *¼ teaspoon* salt
- *2 ⅓ cups (440g)* dark muscovado sugar or brown sugar
- *2 sticks (230g)* butter, at room temperature
- *⅔ cup (226g)* molasses
- *4 teaspoons* vanilla bean paste or pure vanilla extract
- *6 teaspoons* freshly-grated ginger
- *3 large* organic eggs
- *2 ripe* bananas, mashed

For the toffee sauce
- *½ cup plus 2 tablespoons (125g)* brown sugar
- *½ cup (120ml)* heavy cream
- *½ cup (115g) or 1 stick* unsalted butter
- *2 tablespoons* molasses
- *1 teaspoon* vanilla bean paste or pure vanilla extract

For the meringue buttercream
- *4 large* organic eggs whites
- *1 cup (200g)* sugar
- *1 teaspoon* vanilla bean paste or pure vanilla extract
- *1 ¼ cups (280g)* unsalted butter, at room temperature and cut into cubes

*T*his is another cake that is sure to impress! I had an amazing sticky toffee cake at a cafè in London, where I have spent many lovely Christmases back in the day. So, I have finally come up with my own version. I love the name "sticky toffee," don't you? It makes me think of something decadent, gooey, sweet, dense, and aromatic. This cake has it all! It's meant to be presented on a stand and shared with friends and loved ones.*

Method

Preheat the oven to 350°F (180°C). Butter 2 8-inch (20-cm) round cake pans and line the bottoms with parchment paper.

In a medium-sized saucepan, combine the dates and 1 ¼ cups (300 ml) of water and bring to a boil. Continue boiling until the dates are soft, then transfer the dates to a food processor or blender and blend until puréed. Let cool to room temperature.

In a large bowl, sift together the flour, baking powder, cinnamon, nutmeg, and salt.

In the bowl of a stand mixer fitted with the paddle attachment, beat the muscovado sugar and butter until fluffy. Add the molasses, vanilla, and ginger, and beat for 1 minute. Add the eggs, 1 at a time, beating on low until fully incorporated. Add the mashed bananas and the date purée and beat until combined.

Add the flour mixture and beat until just combined. Divide the batter between the prepared pans and bake for 35 to 40 minutes, or until a toothpick inserted in the center comes out clean. Let the cakes cool in the pans for about 30 minutes, then invert them onto a wire rack and let cool completely.

Make the toffee sauce in a medium-sized saucepan by combining the brown sugar, cream, butter, molasses, and vanilla and bringing to a boil. Continue boiling for about 2 minutes until thickened. Remove from the heat and whisk the sauce.

While the cakes are still warm, but not too hot, prick the tops all over with a wooden skewer or toothpick. Reserve about half of the toffee sauce for decoration, then pour the rest over the cakes.

Make the meringue buttercream in a metal bowl set over a pan of simmering water by combining the egg whites and sugar and cook, whisking constantly, until the sugar is fully dissolved and the mixture reaches 160°F (71°C). Transfer to the bowl of a stand mixer fitted with the whisk attachment and whip on medium-high until the bowl is cool to the touch and the egg whites are stiff. Add the vanilla and whip until fully incorporated. Switch to the paddle attachment and with the mixer on low speed, start adding the butter. Continue beating until the buttercream is creamy and shiny. Refrigerate the buttercream and allow it to set while you prepare the cake.

Arrange 1 cake layer on a cake board or serving plate and spread an even layer of buttercream on top. Place the other cake layer on top of the buttercream, then cover the top and sides of the cake with a thin layer of buttercream. Refrigerate for at least 1 hour to set.

If the toffee sauce is too thick, warm it slightly, but not too much or it will melt the buttercream. Using a spoon, drizzle some of the sauce around the edges of the cake, allowing it drip down the sides, then fill the center with more sauce. Allow the ganache to set at room temperature. Add any additional decorations you like and serve.

Tronchetto Di Natale Al Tiramisù

TIRAMISÙ CHRISTMAS LOG

*I*n my first book, "The Italian Baker" I *presented a cake that became very popular. I couldn't be more grateful to those who choose to make my recipe for their celebrations! And so, seeing how the combination of coffee, mascarpone, and cocoa has proven to be one of the most beloved of all time, I now present my version of a Christmas log, which is another good way to enjoy tiramisù any time of the year! The preparation is, of course, different from my famous layer cake, but it is still amazingly delicious. Be sure to drench the sponge thoroughly to guarantee a full coffee aroma. Since I wish to make your life easier, I again decided not to use raw eggs for the filling, so there's no need to temper them. I am assuming you already have enough to cook and bake during the holidays, right? This recipe requires little effort, but is always successful. Also, as there are no raw eggs, this recipe is safe for mums-to-be, too!*

Ingredients

6/8 servings

For the cake
- *¾ cup* plus *1 tablespoon (110g)* all-purpose flour
- *1 teaspoon* baking powder
- *¼ teaspoon* salt
- *5 large organic eggs, separated*
- *½ cup* plus *1 tablespoon (110g)* granulated sugar
- *1 teaspoon* vanilla bean paste or pure vanilla extract

For the mascarpone filling
- *10 ounces (250g)* mascarpone cheese, preferably firm and cold
- *¼ cup* plus *2 tablespoons (40g)* confectioners' sugar
- *1 cup* plus *1 tablespoon (250ml)* double whipping cream
- *2 tablespoons* plus *1 to 2 teaspoons (35 to 40ml)* brewed espresso coffee, cold
- *Unsweetened cocoa powder, to decorate*

Method

Preheat the oven to 350°F (180°C) and line a baking sheet with parchment paper. Wet the parchment with water, then squeeze out the water and lay the parchment back on the baking sheet.

Make the sponge cake in a large bowl. Sift the flour twice, then add the baking powder and salt and sift again.

In the bowl of a stand mixer fitted with the whisk attachment, whip the egg yolks and granulated sugar on medium speed until tripled in volume.

In a large bowl, use a hand-held mixer to whip the egg whites until stiff. Fold them into the egg yolk mixture using very gentle movements starting from the bottom and going upwards. Add the flour mixture and use the same gentle folding method until it is thoroughly combined. Gently fold in the vanilla.

Using an offset spatula, gently spread the batter over the entire surface of the prepared baking sheet. Bake for about 10 minutes or until lightly golden on the edges. Allow to cool to room temperature on the baking sheet.

Wet and squeeze out a second sheet of parchment paper, then lay it on top of the baked cake. With the parchment used during baking, flip the cake upside down onto a work surface, then peel off the parchment. Starting on the shorter end, roll up the cake into a log and wrap it in a barely humid kitchen cloth. Let cool completely.

Make the mascarpone filling in a medium-sized bowl, stir together the mascarpone and confectioners' sugar until just combined.

In the bowl of a stand mixture fitted with the whisk attachment or using a hand-held mixer, whip the cream until medium-stiff peaks form. Fold the cream into the mascarpone mixture, then refrigerate for 10 minutes to set.

Unroll the sponge cake on a work surface, removing the kitchen cloth and the remaining parchment. Pour the cold coffee over the entire surface and let it absorb for about 3 minutes. Spread the mascarpone filling over the entire surface of the cake. Starting on the shorter end, roll up the cake into a log and arrange on a serving plate. Using a fork, create waves over the surface, then dust with the cocoa powder. Decorate with berries or mistletoe (if desired), and serve.

Paris-Brest

Ingredients

10 servings

For the pâte à choux
- *½ cup (130ml)* whole milk
- *¼ cup (60g)* unsalted butter
- *1 teaspoon* confectioners' sugar
- Pinch of salt
- *½ cup (65g)* bread flour (alternatively, Manitoba flour), sifted
- *4 ounces (100g)* eggs (about 2 large eggs)

For the egg wash
- *1 extra large organic egg
- *2 tablespoons* whole milk

To decorate
- *4 ounces (100g)* sliced almonds
- *½ teaspoon* confectioners' sugar

For the crème mousseline
- *5 ¾ ounces (145g)* hazelnut brittle (for instructions see p. 42)
- *1 cup plus 3 tablespoons (350ml)* whole milk
- *1 teaspoon* vanilla bean paste or pure vanilla extract
- *3 large organic eggs
- *1 ¼ cups plus 1 tablespoon (140g)* confectioners' sugar
- *⅓ cup plus 2 tablespoons (55g)* all-purpose flour
- *1 cup plus 2 tablespoons (255g)* unsalted butter, at room temperature

*P*aris-Brest was originally created to celebrate a bicycle race starting from Paris, passing through Brest, and returning back to Paris. This is the reason for its round shape, resembling the wheel of a bike. Over the years, Paris-Brest has become one of the most popular desserts around the world. You can make small individual portions or one large cake like this one, which looks stunning in the center of the table. For those who are not familiar with pâte à choux, don't be afraid to give it a try—it's not as difficult as it sounds. This is the traditional version, but once you master the technique, you can play with different flavors like coffee or seasonal fruits. Either way, this feather-light dessert will not disappoint you.

Method

Preheat the oven to 375°F (190°C). Cut a sheet of parchment paper into a 9 ½-inch (24-cm) round and set on a baking sheet.

Make the pâte à choux in a medium-sized saucepan set over medium heat, combining the milk, butter, sugar, and salt and bringing it to a boil. Remove from the heat, add the sifted bread flour, and stir vigorously with a wooden spoon until the flour is fully incorporated and a film forms on the back of the spoon. Transfer to the bowl of a stand mixer fitted with the paddle attachment and beat on low for 1 minute. Meanwhile, in a separate bowl, whisk the eggs, then gradually add them to the batter until fully incorporated. Turn the mixer to high and beat for 3 minutes, or until fully combined.

Transfer the mixture to a piping bag fitted with a medium round piping tip (14-mm round, 11-mm star tip or number 846 Ateco brand) and pipe a circle onto the round template you created earlier. Pipe a sec-

ond circle inside the first one, then pipe a third circle in between (on top of) the first 2 circles. In a small bowl, quickly whisk together the egg and milk. Using a pastry brush, brush the entire surface with some egg wash.

Sprinkle the flaked almonds and confectioners' sugar over the circles and bake, without opening the oven door, for about 20 minutes, or until the "crown" is fully baked and golden on top. Let cool completely.

Make the crème mousseline in a medium-sized bowl and using a hand-held electric mixer on high, pulse the hazelnut brittle until a creamy paste forms.

In a medium-sized saucepan over medium heat, stir together the milk and vanilla and bring to a gentle simmer. Meanwhile, crack the eggs into a bowl and add the sugar. Stir quickly by hand using a hand whisk. Add the flour and whisk again. Once the milk mixture is gently boiling, pour it over the egg mixture and quickly whisk. Return to the stove and cook, stirring constantly for about 3 minutes until thick. Pour into a bowl, cover with plastic wrap, and refrigerate until cold.

Once the mousseline is cold, whisk until creamy again. Add the hazelnut paste and the room temperature butter and stir until fully incorporated. Cover with plastic wrap and refrigerate until ready to use.

Cut the Paris-Brest horizontally in half. Quickly stir the crème mousseline, then transfer to a piping bag fitted with a star-shaped tip or another tip and pipe rosettes around the base of the Paris-Brest. Place the top of the Paris-Brest on the crème mousseline and dust with some confectioners' sugar.

Mont Blanc

The Mont Blanc is one of those miraculous preparations that leaves me astonished every time I see it, eat it, or make it. Whoever created this dessert, which resembles the Mont Blanc mountain that divides Italy and France, has a dear place in my heart. A good Mont Blanc needs to be light in texture, sweet in flavor, and beautiful in appearance. And Christmas is the perfect time of year to make one. Follow the recipe closely and you will not fail. I have made it easy because I refuse to spend too much time making something when I am in a rush to eat it. It's a question of priorities, and I know mine!

Ingredients

Makes about 50 (1 ¼-inch / 3-cm) meringues and about 8 servings

For the meringues
- 3 medium organic egg whites, at room temperature
- ¼ teaspoon cream of tartar
- 1 ¼ cups (130g) confectioners' sugar, sifted
- 1 teaspoon freshly-squeezed, organic lemon juice

For the Mont Blanc
- 24 ounces (600g) chestnut purée
- 2 tablespoons (30g) unsalted butter, at room temperature
- 1 tablespoon plus 1 teaspoon (20ml) rum
- 1 teaspoon unsweetened cocoa powder
- 2 cups plus 1 tablespoon (495ml) double whipping cream
- 8 ounces (200g) small chocolate chips
- 5 marron glacés, roughly chopped

Method

Preheat the oven to 175°F (80°C) and line a baking sheet with parchment paper.

Make the meringues in the bowl of a stand mixer fitted with the whisk attachment or by using a hand-held mixer. Combine the egg whites and cream of tartar, then whip on medium until frothy. Add the confectioners' sugar in 3 additions and whip until fully incorporated. Add the lemon juice and whip until stiff. Transfer to a piping bag fitted with a round tip (2A) and pipe 1 ¼-inch (3-cm) rounds onto the parchment-lined baking sheet. If you are not confident with your piping skills, use a pencil and a 1 ¼-inch (3-cm) round cookie cutter to draw circles on the parchment, then flip it upside down to avoid contact between the pencil mark and the meringues. Bake without opening the oven door, so the meringues don't deflate, for about 90 minutes or until light to the touch. Turn the oven off, but leave the meringues inside and let cool completely.

Make the Mont Blanc in a large bowl by combining 16 ounces (400g) of the chestnut purée with the butter, rum, and cocoa powder. Stir until a paste forms, then cover and refrigerate until ready to use.

In the bowl of a stand mixer fitted with the whisk attachment, whip the cream until medium-stiff peaks form. Gently fold about one-third of the whipped cream into the remaining 8 ounces (200g) of chestnut purée.

Arrange an 8 to 9-inch (20 to 23-cm) round cake board or serving plate on a work surface. Spread a layer of the chestnut whipped cream on the cake board to create a base for the meringues, then add a layer of meringues. Top with chocolate chips and pieces of marron glacès. Repeat to create more layers and build a tall dome or pyramid shape with the chestnut whipped cream, meringues, chocolate chips, and marrons glacès. Using a spatula, spread more chestnut whipped cream over the cake, then use a spatula to cover the cake with the remaining pure whipped cream, making it as smooth as possible.

Remove the chestnut mixture from the refrigerator. It should be quite stiff, but if it's too loose, add a little more cocoa powder and place it back in the refrigerator to set. Transfer to a piping bag fitted with a small round tip and pipe circles around the entire surface of the Mont Blanc. Alternatively, use a potato ricer, allowing the chestnut mixture to drop in irregular strips over the cake to create the famous Mont Blanc motif. Top with additional pieces of marron glacès, meringues, or bits of gold leaf for a more luxurious finish. Refrigerate for about 1 hour and remove 30 minutes before serving.

Torta Al Profumo Di Natale

CHRISTMAS-SCENTED CAKE

Egg Free Dairy Free!

Ingredients

6/8 servings

- *1 ¾ ounces (45g)* dried dates, pitted and chopped
- *2 tablespoons* clear liquid honey
- *2 ¾ cups (355g)* sifted all-purpose flour (preferably unbleached)
- *½ teaspoon* baking soda
- *½ teaspoon* baking powder
- Pinch of salt
- *1 cup (230g)* muscovado sugar
- *2 tablespoons* golden syrup
- *4 teaspoons* freshly-grated ginger
- *1 teaspoon* ground cinnamon
- *1 teaspoon* vanilla bean paste or pure vanilla extract
- *¼ teaspoon* ground nutmeg
- *½ cup (120ml)* vegetable oil
- *1 teaspoon* brandy
- *1 ⅓ cup plus 1 tablespoon (100ml)* water, at room temperature
- *1 ½ ounces (40g)* dried apricots, chopped

*T*his is the closest thing I know to a traditional English Christmas fruitcake—dense, packed with dried fruit, and full of amazing flavor. However, as opposed to the English version, this one doesn't require a long time to make. There's more good news: It's egg and dairy free!

A little tip: You can drench the cake with a simple syrup made by bringing equal parts sugar and water, plus some freshly-squeezed orange juice, to a boil. Let the syrup cool, then brush it over the warm cake and wait for the magic to happen! This cake smells like pure Christmas to me!!

Method

Preheat the oven to 350°F (180°C) and line the bottom of a deep 8 x 6 ¼-inch (20 x 15.5-cm) cake pan with parchment paper.

In a food processor or blender, combine the dates and honey and blend until reduced to a paste.

In a large bowl, combine the flour, baking soda, baking powder, and salt.

In the bowl of a stand mixer fitted with the paddle attachment, combine the muscovado sugar, golden syrup, ginger, cinnamon, vanilla, and nutmeg, then beat until the sugar is fully coated in the spices and smells fantastic. Add the vegetable oil and brandy and beat until combined. Add the date paste and beat until incorporated, then add the water and beat until thoroughly mixed in. Add the flour mixture and beat until combined. Fold in the chopped apricots, then pour into the prepared pan and bake for about 40 minutes, or until a toothpick inserted in the center comes out clean. Once baked, leave the cake in the pan for about 30 minutes before inverting it onto a wire rack. Allow to cool at room temperature before serving.

Semifreddo Alle Nocciole Pralinate

HAZELNUT PRALINE SEMIFREDDO

Ingredients

About 8/10 servings

For the hazelnut praline (brittle)
- *3 ¼ ounces (82g)* whole blanched hazelnuts
- *¼ cup* plus *2 tablespoons (80g)* sugar

For the pâte à bombe
- *¾ cup (150g)* sugar
- *3 ¼ ounces (82g)* large egg yolks (preferably super fresh and organic)

For the Italian meringue
- *¾ cup (150g)* sugar
- *2 ¼ ounces (60g)* organic egg whites

For the semifreddo
- *1 cup (250ml)* heavy cream
- *10 ounces (250g)* mascarpone cheese

To decorate
- *4 ounces (100g)* chopped chocolate or melted chocolate chips
- Whole blanched hazelnuts

*S*emifreddo means something like "almost cold," but not quite. It's not ice cream, nor is it a cold pudding. Semifreddo really deserves a place of its own in the world of pastry. It can be served any time of year, and the flavor combinations are endless—in summer, let your creativity go wild with all the fruit available. For the holiday season, hazelnuts are a must, though you can add other ingredients in the form of a paste, such as marron glacés or chocolate. For Christmas, the most beautiful time of year, this semifreddo is a classic. It will be the perfect ending to a perfect meal.

Note: This recipe provides more meringue than will you actually need, but it is very hard to work with less than two egg whites, as they will not whip properly. Any leftover meringue can be kept in the fridge for about 2 days or used for decorating any other cake you like.

Method

Make the hazelnut praline by toasting the hazelnuts in a large skillet over medium heat, shaking the pan occasionally, for about 5 minutes or until medium golden. Line a large plate with parchment paper and place the toasted hazelnuts in the middle, trying to keep them close together rather than spread out.

In a medium-sized saucepan over low-medium heat, melt about half of the sugar without stirring. Be careful, as the sugar gets really hot! Once the sugar is completely melted, stir it with a wooden spoon and add the rest of the sugar. Continue cooking until golden in color. Carefully pour the hot caramel over the hazelnuts. Let sit at room temperature until cool to the touch, then refrigerate until completely set. Transfer to a food processor and grind to a fine texture.

Make the pâte à bombe in a medium-sized saucepan over medium heat, by combining the sugar and 3 tablespoons (45 ml) of water. Cook without stirring, until the sugar is completely melted.

While the sugar syrup is cooking, in the bowl of a stand mixer fitted with the whisk attachment, whip the egg yolks until pale.

→

Once the syrup reaches 250°F (120°C), with the mixer on low, very carefully pour it over the egg yolks in a steady stream and whip until fully incorporated. Continue whipping until the mixture is even paler in color and doubled in volume. Refrigerate until ready to use.

Make the Italian meringue in a medium-sized saucepan over medium heat by combining the sugar and ¼ cup (60 ml) of water. Cook without stirring, until the sugar is completely melted.

While the sugar syrup is cooking, in the bowl of a stand mixer fitted with the whisk attachment, whip the egg yolks until pale.

Once the syrup reaches 250°F (120°C), with the mixer on low, very carefully pour it over the egg whites in a steady stream and whip until fully incorporated. Continue whipping until the mixture has a marshmallow-like consistency.

Make the semifreddo in the bowl of a stand mixer fitted with the whisk attachment or using a hand-held mixer. Whip the cream until medium-stiff peaks form.

In a large bowl, whisk the mascarpone cheese until creamy. Add a small amount of the pâte à bombe and stir until smooth and creamy. Add the rest of the pâte à bombe and stir until smooth and creamy. Add the hazelnut praline and stir to combine. Gradually and gently fold in half of the Italian meringue, then gently fold in the whipped cream. Pour the semifreddo into 1 large or several small freezer-safe molds and freeze for at least 5 hours.

In a bain-marie or a metal bowl set over a pan of simmering water, melt the chocolate. Remove from the heat and let cool—it has to be liquid, but not too warm or it will melt your semifreddo. Remove the semifreddo from the freezer, unmold it, and place it on a serving plate. Pour the chocolate over the semifreddo, sprinkle with hazelnuts and serve immediately.

Eggnog Orange Layer Cake

Ingredients

About 12 slices

For the cake
- *2 ½ cups (325g)* all-purpose flour, sifted
- *4 teaspoons* baking powder
- *1 teaspoon* ground cinnamon
- *1 teaspoon* ground nutmeg
- *2 ¼ cups (450g)* granulated sugar
- *7 large* organic eggs
- *2 teaspoons* vanilla bean paste or pure vanilla extract
- *1 cup plus 1 tablespoon (240g)* unsalted butter, melted and cooled to room temperature
- *1 ½ cups plus 2 tablespoons (390ml)* eggnog (see recipe at page 112)

For the filling
- *13 ounces (320g)* orange marmalade

For the frosting
- *2 cups plus 1 tablespoon (500ml)* heavy whipping cream, chilled
- *2 tablespoons* confectioners' sugar

*O*ne either loves or hates eggnog, and I am firmly a fan of this boozy, creamy drink that smells sooooo good! Are you in need of a great centerpiece that shouts, "Christmas"? Look no further because here you have it! My eggnogg orange layer cake is easy to make and fun to decorate in any way you like. I strongly suggest to go overboard and kitsch! Yeah! Why not? It's so much fun!

Method

Preheat the oven to 350°F (180°C). Butter 2 8-inch (20-cm) round cake pans and line the bottoms with parchment paper.

Make the cake batter by whisking together the flour, baking powder, cinnamon, and nutmeg in a large bowl.

In the bowl of a stand mixer fitted with a paddle attachment or using a hand-held mixer, beat the granulated sugar and eggs on high until doubled in volume and very pale. Add the vanilla. With the mixer on low, add the melted butter in a slow, steady stream and mix until fully incorporated, being careful not to mix it too much. Add the eggnog and beat until incorporated. Add the flour and spices mixture in 3 ad-

ditions and fold by hand until incorporated. Pour the batter into the prepared pans and bake for about 40 minutes, or until a toothpick inserted in the center of the cake comes out clean. Let the cakes cool in the pans for about 20 minutes, then invert onto a wire rack to cool completely.

Place 1 cake layer on a cake board or serving platter. Using a long serrated knife, slice the layer horizontally in half. Repeat with the second cake layer. You should have 4 cake layers.

Make the frosting in the bowl of a stand mixer fitted with the whisk attachment. Whip the heavy whipping cream and confectioners' sugar until stiff peaks form. Transfer to a piping bag, fill it halfway, then cut the tip with a pair of scissors. Pipe a circle of frosting around the edge of the first cake layer and fill the center with orange marmalade. Repeat with the remaining cake layers, frosting, and marmalade until there are 4 cake layers with jam filling. Spread the remaining frosting on the sides and top of the cake and decorate as you please with gingerbread cookies, or sprinkle all over with glitter for a sparkly holiday cake! Your creativity will be appreciated by your guests!

Bavarese Doppio Cioccolato

DOUBLE CHOCOLATE BAVARIAN CREAM

Ingredients

Serves up to 10 people

For the milk chocolate
Bavarian cream

- *8 ounces (200g)* milk chocolate, roughly chopped
- *1 ¼ cups (300ml)* whole milk
- *¾ cup* plus *1 tablespoon (200ml)* heavy cream
- *2 tablespoons (20g)* sugar
- *1 teaspoon* vanilla bean paste
- *2 teaspoons* agar agar powder

For the dark chocolate
Bavarian cream

- *8 ounces (200g)* good quality dark chocolate, roughly chopped
- *1 ¼ cups (300ml)* whole milk
- *¾ cup* plus *1 tablespoon (200ml)* heavy cream
- *2 tablespoons (20g)* sugar
- *1 teaspoon* vanilla bean paste
- *2 teaspoons* agar agar powder

*E*very fancy dinner requires a fancy dessert, so if you are about to organize a stylish and glamorous dinner party, this is the recipe for you. I don't use animal-based gelatin in my desserts and this is no exception. Agar agar powder sometimes creates a less than super fine texture in the cream, but I am a firm believer that you can't always get what you want. What's more, because I have strong principles, I would rather stick to them and avoid animal gelatin, which is often poorly sourced. Besides, the recipe is delicious and I personally have no problem with the texture. I am using a pudding mold or bundt cake mold for this, but feel free to use any mold you like. You can double or triple the recipe according to the number of guests invited and the size of your mold.

Method

For the milk chocolate bavarois, place the mold in the freezer. In a bain-marie or a metal bowl set over a pan of simmering water, melt the milk chocolate. Once melted, set each aside.

In a medium-sized saucepan, combine the milk, heavy cream, sugar, vanilla, and agar agar powder. Place over medium heat and bring to a temperature of 175°F (85°C),

while whisking constantly, then remove from the heat. Add the melted chocolate and stir until fully incorporated.

Remove the mold from the freezer and pour in the milk chocolate mixture. Leave at room temperature to set for 30 minutes, then chill in the freezer for 2 hours.

For the dark chocolate Bavarian cream, melt the dark chocolate in a bain-marie or a metal bowl set over a pan of simmering water. Repeat the same process using dark chocolate.

In a medium-sized saucepan, combine the milk, heavy cream, sugar, vanilla, and agar agar powder. Place over medium heat and bring to a temperature of 175°F (85°C) while whisking constantly, then remove from the heat. Leave at room temperature to set for about 15 minutes (the dark chocolate needs less time than the milk chocolate).

Remove the mold from the freezer and pour the dark chocolate mixture over the frozen milk chocolate mixture. Return the mold to the freezer and chill overnight.

When ready to serve, quickly blowtorch the sides of the mold or dip it in hot water to release the Bavarian cream, then invert it onto a serving plate.

Red Velvet Cake

Ingredients

12 servings

For the cake

- *3 ½ cups (440g)* organic all-purpose flour, sifted
- *2 cups* plus *5 tablespoons (300g)* white granulated beet sugar
- *1 tablespoon* vegan unsweetened cocoa powder
- *2 teaspoons* baking soda
- *½ teaspoon* salt
- *2 cups (480ml)* almond milk or other dairy-free milk
- *⅔ cup (150ml)* organic non-GMO vegetable oil
- *2 tablespoons* natural red food coloring
- *2 ½ teaspoons* vanilla bean paste or pure vanilla extract

For the frosting

- *1 cup* plus *1 tablespoon (250g)* vegan butter
- *20 ounces (500g)* spreadable vegan cream cheese
- *1 ½ teaspoons* vanilla bean paste or pure vanilla extract
- *2 cups (240g)* vegan confectioners' sugar

*R*ed velvet cake made vegan? YES! There is no reason to give up on a good slice of Red Velvet only because it's vegan. This cake quickly sells out at my shop. People simply love it. Plus, it's red, so it's perfect for the holidays! Bear in mind that you must use 100% natural food coloring. Red food coloring is typically made using lady bug pigments, so it's not vegetarian and it's certainly not vegan. I'm not a big fan of butter substitutes, as I feel they are not natural, but to make this recipe vegan, I had to give in. The same goes for vegan cream cheese. If you wish to keep this cake as healthy as possible, skip the cream cheese and make a bare cake, perhaps dusted with a little vegan confectioners' sugar. I know this recipe will make many of you very happy! You have been requesting it for quite a while now, and so this is my little Christmas gift to you. Even if you are not vegan, this recipe is for you, too. I hope you will bake it over and over!

Method

Preheat oven to 350°F (180°C). Brush vegetable oil on the bottom and sides of 2 8-inch (20-cm) round cake pans line the bottoms with parchment paper.

Make the cake in a large bowl by whisking together the flour, white granulated beet sugar, cocoa powder, baking soda, and salt.

In a medium-sized bowl, whisk together the almond milk, vegetable oil, red food coloring, and vanilla, then pour into the middle of the flour mixture and stir to combine, but do not overmix. Divide the cake batter between the prepared pans and bake for 35 to 40 minutes, or until a toothpick inserted in the center comes out clean. Let the cakes cool before removing them from the pans.

Make the frosting in the bowl of a stand mixer fitted with the paddle attachment. Beat the vegan butter on low until creamy. With the mixer on low, slowly add the spreadable vegan cream cheese and vanilla and beat until combined. Add the vegan confectioners' sugar and beat until fully combined. If the frosting is too dry, add a few drops of almond milk.

Arrange 1 cake layer on a cake board or serving plate and cover with a layer of frosting. Place the other cake layer on top of the frosting, then cover the top and sides of the cake with the remaining frosting. Refrigerate for about 30 minutes to set, then cut into slices and serve.

Torta Alla Crema Di Nocciole

HAZELNUT CHOCOLATE CAKE

Ingredients

12 Servings

For the cake
- *3 ½ ounces (90g)* good quality dark chocolate (minimum 65% cacao), cut into small pieces
- *⅔ cup plus 2 teaspoons (160ml)* hot brewed coffee
- *2 ⅓ cups (300g)* all-purpose flour, sifted
- *1 cup (100g)* unsweetened cocoa powder
- *2 teaspoons* baking soda
- *1 teaspoon* baking powder
- *2 ¾ cups (550g)* sugar
- *¼ teaspoon* salt
- *4* large organic eggs, at room temperature
- *1 ½ cups (360ml)* buttermilk, at room temperature
- *⅔ cup plus 1 tablespoon plus 1 teaspoon (170ml)* vegetable oil
- *2 tablespoons* hazelnut liqueur, such as Frangelico
- *1 teaspoon* vanilla bean paste or pure vanilla extract
- *12 ounces (300g)* good quality hazelnut chocolate spread

For the hazelnut Swiss meringue buttercream
- *8* large organic egg whites, at room temperature
- *2 ½ cups (500g)* sugar
- *¼ teaspoon* salt
- *3 cups plus 2 teaspoons (700g)* unsalted butter, at room temperature and cut into cubes
- *3 tablespoons* good quality hazelnut chocolate spread

To decorate
- *6 ounces (150g)* good quality dark chocolate (minimum 65% cacao)
- Whole blanched hazelnuts

*T*his is a stunning layer cake and guaranteed to impress. I suggest you make it for a New Year's Eve party and decorate it with lots of lights or even candles—why not? This cake deserves a place of honor on your table. It was born a star!

Note: For better results, the Swiss meringue buttercream recipe produces more than you actually need. But you can store the buttercream in the fridge for up to 3 days, or freeze it for up to 1 month. Plus, I believe it's always good to have a little extra buttercream on hand for decorating. When adding the butter, make sure it's at room temperature. If it's too warm, it will melt the buttercream, and if it's too cold, it will curdle the buttercream. To test, pinch the butter with your fingers—if you leave a print, it's the right temperature.

Method

Preheat the oven to 350°F (180°C). Spray 2 8-inch (20-cm) round cake pans with baking spray and line the bottoms with parchment paper.

Make the cake batter in a medium-sized bowl by combining the chocolate and hot brewed coffee, then stir to melt the chocolate. Let cool slightly at room temperature.

In a large bowl, sift together the flour, cocoa powder, baking soda, and baking powder. Add the sugar and salt and whisk to combine.

In the bowl of a stand mixer fitted with the paddle attachment or using a hand-held mixer, beat the eggs on medium until frothy. Add the buttermilk, oil, hazelnut liqueur, and vanilla and beat for about 1 minute or until combined. Add the cooled chocolate mixture and beat until incorporated. Add the flour mixture in 3 additions, beating after each one until combined. Divide the batter between the prepared pans and bake for 45 to 50 minutes, or until a toothpick inserted in the center comes out clean. Let the cakes cool in the pans for about 15 minutes, then invert onto a wire rack to cool completely.

→

Make the hazelnut Swiss meringue buttercream in a metal bowl set over a pan of simmering water. Combine the egg whites, sugar, and salt, whisking constantly, until the sugar is fully dissolved and the mixture reaches 160°F (71°C). Transfer to the bowl of a stand mixer fitted with the whisk attachment and whip on medium-high until the bowl is cool to the touch and the egg whites are stiff. Switch to the paddle attachment and with the mixer on low speed, start adding the butter. Continue beating until the buttercream is creamy and shiny. Add

the hazelnut chocolate spread and beat until fully combined and glossy. Refrigerate the buttercream so it will set while you prepare the cake.

Arrange 1 cake layer on a cake board or serving plate and spread an even layer of the chocolate hazelnut spread on top. Place the other cake layer on top of the chocolate hazelnut spread, then cover the top and sides of the cake with a thin layer of the hazelnut Swiss meringue buttercream. There is no need to be precise at this point, as you are giving the cake what is called a

"crumb coating." Refrigerate the cake for 15 minutes to set. Spread a second layer of the buttercream on the top and sides of the cake. Using a cake scraper, remove excess buttercream to reveal the cake underneath. This step, called crumb coating, is necessary in order to seal any crumbs and to build a smooth surface. Then frost the cake entirely with the buttercream (reserving some to pipe decorations on at the end). Refrigerate for about 30 minutes to set.

In a bain-marie or a metal bowl set over a pan of simmering water, melt the dark chocolate. Carefully pour some of the melted chocolate around the sides of the cake, then refrigerate to set for about 5 minutes. Carefully pour some of the melted chocolate on top of the cake and let set at room temperature or in the fridge. Fill a piping bag fitted with an open star tip with buttercream and pipe rosettes on top of the cake. Top each rosette with a hazelnut, cut the cake into slices, and serve. Your cake will be stunning—I am absolutely sure!

Tangerine Curd Cake

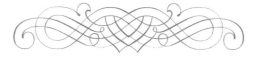

Ingredients

10/12 servings

For the cake
- *3 cups* plus *1 tablespoon (400g)* all-purpose flour
- *2 tablespoons* baking powder
- *4* large organic eggs
- *1 ¼ cups plus 1 tablespoon (265g)* sugar
- *2 teaspoons* vanilla bean paste or pure vanilla extract
- *1 ⅔ cups (400ml)* chilled double whipping cream
- Freshly-grated zest of *2* organic tangerines
- Freshly-grated zest of *1* organic lemon

For the tangerine curd
- *6* large organic egg yolks
- *½ cup* plus *2 tablespoons (120g)* sugar
- *½ cup (120ml)* freshly-squeezed tangerine juice
- *3 teaspoons* freshly-grated, organic tangerine zest
- *1 tablespoon* organic cornstarch
- *⅓ cup* plus *2 teaspoons (85g)* unsalted butter, cold and cut into cubes

For the chantilly cream
- *2 cups* plus *1 tablespoon (500ml)* chilled double whipping cream
- *3 tablespoons* confectioners' sugar

To decorate
- White chocolate shavings
- Gold leaves (optional)
- Tangerines, peeled and unpeeled

*T*he flavor of citrus fruits is never too much. This is my opinion. I remember spending Christmas in the countryside and during lazy afternoons, after a big lunch, my uncle would eat a tangerine or two and throw pieces of the peel into the fireplace. As a child, I used to hate that smell. It's funny how we change as we grow up. What used to be so unpleasant is now one of my favorite things in the world. Tangerines are juicy and fresh, and I think they should be used more often in the kitchen and not only for dessert. Here is a recipe that will make you the queen or king of the holidays!

Method

Preheat the oven to 350°F (180°C). Line 2 8-inch (20-cm) round cake pans with parchment paper.

In a large bowl, sift together the flour and baking powder.

In the bowl of a stand mixer fitted with the whisk attachment, combine the eggs and sugar and whip until doubled in volume and very pale. Add the vanilla and whip to combine. Add the flour mixture and gently fold until fully incorporated

In a large bowl, use an electric mixer to whip the cream until stiff peaks form. Fold into the batter, then add the tangerine and lemon zest and stir to combine. Pour into the prepared pans and bake for 40 to 45 minutes, or until a toothpick inserted in the center comes out clean. Let cool in the pans, then invert onto a wire rack and let cool completely.

Make the tangerine curd in a medium-sized saucepan over medium heat. Whisk together the egg yolks, sugar, tangerine juice and zest, and cornstarch. Stir constantly until the mixture is thick. Remove from the heat and whisk in the butter. Cover with plastic wrap and refrigerate until completely cool.

Make the chantilly cream in the bowl of a stand mixer fitted with the whisk attachment. Whip cream and confectioners' sugar until stiff peaks form.

Arrange 1 cake layer on a cake board or serving plate and spread an even layer of tangerine curd on top. Place the other cake layer on top of the curd, then cover the top and sides of the cake with the chantilly cream. Decorate as you wish, with white chocolate shavings, gold leaves (optional), and peeled and unpeeled tangerines. Cut into slices and serve.

Winter Coconut Cake

Ingredients

12 servings

For the cake
- *3 cups (380g)* all-purpose flour
- *1 ½ cups (168g)* almond flour
- *4 teaspoons* baking powder
- *½ teaspoon* salt
- *1 ⅓ cups plus 2 tablespoons plus 2 teaspoons (340g)* unsalted butter, at room temperature
- *3 cups (600g)* granulated sugar
- *6 large* organic eggs
- *2 teaspoons* vanilla bean paste or pure vanilla extract
- *3 drops* pure almond extract (optional)
- *1 ½ cups (360ml)* buttermilk, at room temperature

For the syrup
- *1 cup (200g)* granulated sugar
- *2 tablespoons* rum (optional)

For the ganache filling
- *8 ounces (200g)* white chocolate
- *1 cup plus 2 teaspoons (250ml)* heavy cream
- *10 ounces (250g)* mascarpone cheese (preferably firm)
- *⅓ cup plus 1 tablespoon plus 1 teaspoon (100ml)* coconut milk, chilled
- *cup (50g)* shredded coconut
- *2 ounces (50g)* crushed almonds

To decorate
- *2 ⅓ cups (500ml)* double whipping cream
- *1 tablespoon* confectioners' sugar
- *½ cup (50g)* shredded coconut
- Coconut chocolates

*T*his gorgeous cake, white as snow, is made with almonds, coconut, and a hint of rum, the ingredients used to make pralines, the famous candy we all know and love. There are so many decoration options that it's hard for me to even think about them. If you prefer to spend your time eating rather than decorating, leave the cake plain and simple and it will look gorgeous. Ready? Roll up your sleeves and let's get baking!

Method

Preheat the oven to 350°F (175°C). Spray 2 8-inch (20-cm) round cake pans with baking spray and line the bottoms with parchment paper.

Make the cake in a large bowl. Whisk together the all-purpose flour, almond flour, baking powder, and salt.

In the bowl of a stand mixer fitted with the paddle attachment, beat the butter and sugar until pale.

Add the eggs, 1 at a time, scraping down the sides of the bowl after each addition. Add the vanilla and almond extract (if using) and beat until combined. Add the flour mixture and the buttermilk in 3 additions, starting and ending with the flour mixture. Divide the batter between the prepared pans and bake for about 40 minutes, or until a wooden toothpick inserted in the center of the cakes comes out clean. Let the cakes cool in the pans for 15 minutes, then invert onto a wire rack to cool completely.

Make the syrup in a small saucepan by combining the sugar, rum (if using), and ¾ cup plus 1 tablespoon plus 1 teaspoon (200 ml) of water and bring to a boil. Remove from the heat.

Make the ganache filling in a bain-marie or a metal bowl set over a pan of simmering water, melt the white chocolate. Let cool at room temperature.

In the bowl of a stand mixer fitted with the whisk attachment, whip the cream until medium-stiff peaks form.

In a medium-sized bowl, combine the mascarpone cheese, chilled coconut milk, shredded coconut, and crushed almonds, and stir until fully combined. Add the melted and cooled white chocolate and gently fold to combine. Add the whipped cream and gently fold to incorporate without overmixing.

Arrange 1 cake layer on a cake board or serving plate. Trim a thin layer of cake off of the top and discard. Brush the entire surface of the cake with the sugar syrup and let soak in for 3 minutes. Spread an even layer of the ganache filling on top of the first cake, then set the second cake layer on top. Spread the remaining ganache in a thin layer on the top and sides of the cake to create a crumb coating. Refrigerate the cake to set for 20 minutes.

In the bowl of a stand mixer fitted with the whisk attachment, whip the cream and confectioners' sugar (for decorating) until stiff peaks form. Using an offset spatula, frost the top and sides of the cake with the whipped cream, smoothing both the top and sides with a cake scraper or spatula if you are more experienced.

Place the shredded coconut in a large bowl. Lift and hold the cake by placing it in the center of one hand, then press the coconut flour along the top and sides until the whole cake is covered and looks like a white cloud. If you wish, you can fill a piping bag fitted with a star tip with leftover whipped cream and pipe rosettes around the top of the cake. Place coconut chocolates on top of the rosettes. Refrigerate the cake until ready to serve.

Torta Cioccolato E Vino Rosso

RED WINE CHOCOLATE CAKE

Ingredients

12 servings

For the cake
- *3 cups* plus *1 tablespoon (400g)* all-purpose flour, sifted
- *¾ cup (75g)* dark unsweetened cocoa powder
- *2 ½ teaspoons* baking soda
- *¼ teaspoon* baking powder
- *¼ teaspoon* salt
- *2 ½ cups (500g)* brown sugar
- *½ cup* plus *1 teaspoon (120g)* unsalted butter, at room temperature
- *⅓ cup* plus *1 tablespoon* plus *1 teaspoon (100ml)* organic vegetable oil
- *6* large organic eggs
- *2 teaspoons* vanilla bean paste or pure vanilla extract
- *1 ¼ cups* plus *3 tablespoons (350ml)* Amarone di Valpolicella Red Wine or Nicolò V Reserve Cantine Lunae

For the chocolate sour cream frosting
- *¾ cup* plus *1 tablespoon (180g)* unsalted butter, at room temperature
- *4 cups (400g)* confectioners' sugar, sifted
- *½ cup (60g)* unsweetened dark cocoa powder
- *7 ounces (180g)* sour cream, at room temperature
- *2 teaspoons* vanilla bean paste or pure vanilla extract

*P*laying with texture, and especially with flavor, is one of the most important and fun things to do in the kitchen. I remember long ago when I was young, and the first chili-infused chocolate bars came on the market. What? Chocolate and chilies? Seriously? It turned out to be one of the most creative flavor combinations. Chocolate, as we all know, is a miraculous ingredient and can be used in myriad ways. Red wine and chocolate is another very unique flavor combination and one that will impress your guests. You'll need a full-bodied wine to enhance the aroma of the chocolate, but this isn't a boozy cake. The wine evaporates during baking, leaving only a wonderful scent in the cake. That means kids will enjoy it, too.

Method

Preheat the oven to 350°F (180°C). Spray 2 8-inch (20-cm) round cake pans and line the bottoms with parchment paper.

Make the cake batter in a large bowl. Sift together the flour, cocoa powder, baking soda, baking powder, and salt.

In the bowl of a stand mixer fitted with the paddle attachment, combine the brown sugar, butter, and oil and beat until creamy. Add the eggs and vanilla and beat until fully combined. Add the flour mixture and the red wine in 3 alternating additions, then beat until fully combined. Divide the batter between the prepared pans and bake for about 40 minutes, or until a wooden toothpick inserted into the center of the cake comes out clean. Let cool in the pans for 15 minutes, then invert onto a wire rack to cool completely.

Make the chocolate sour cream frosting in the bowl of a stand mixer fitted with the paddle attachment. Beat the butter, confectioners' sugar, and cocoa powder until fully combined. Add the sour cream and vanilla and beat on high until smooth and creamy. If the frosting is too runny, add a little more confectioners' sugar.

Arrange 1 cake layer on a cake board or serving plate and cover with a layer of the frosting. Place the other cake layer on top of the frosting, then cover the top and sides of the cake with the remaining frosting. Decorate as you please, then cut into slices and serve.

Torta Verticale Alle Clementine

VERTICAL CLEMENTINE CAKE

Ingredients

About 10 slices

**For the white chocolate
ganache frosting**
- *31 ounces (775g)* white
chocolate, finely chopped
- *1 cup plus 2 teaspoons (250ml)*
double whipping cream

For the cake
- *1 ¾ cups plus 3 tablespoons
plus 2 teaspoons (250g)*
all-purpose flour
- *2 teaspoons* baking powder
- *½ teaspoon* salt
- *8 large organic eggs*
- *1 ½ cups (300g)* granulated
sugar
- *¼ cup plus 2 teaspoons (70g)*
unsalted butter,
melted and cooled
- *1 ½ teaspoons* vanilla bean
paste or pure vanilla extract
- Freshly-grated zest
of *1* organic orange
- *1 jar* clementine marmamlade
(350g)
- *2 cups (200g)* confectioners'
sugar

*H*ow about surprising your guests with
a stunning vertical cake? Those who
know how it's made will be delighted by
your efforts, and those who don't, will be
stunned by how fun it looks! Be prepared
to answer questions, as your cake will be
the star of the Christmas party! I've kept
the ingredients fairly simple, so you can
focus on the technique. But, of course, I
always choose top quality ingredients.
The tangy clementines are balanced by the
sweetness of the white chocolate frosting.
Cakes can be made to fit any occasion, so
keep this recipe on hand for when the season changes and you are in need of another
spectacular cake—simply play with different flavors and seasonal fruits and success
is guaranteed!

*Note: If you wish to color your frosting,
please use only 100 percent natural colors,
which are widely available online.*

Method

Make the white chocolate ganache frosting in a medium-sized, microwave-safe
bowl. Combine the white chocolate and
cream. Melt in 20-second intervals in the
microwave, stirring between each inter-
val. Alternatively, warm the cream in a
saucepan and bring almost to a boil, then
pour over the white chocolate and stir
until melted. Cover with plastic wrap and
let set at room temperature.

Preheat the oven to 350°F (180°C). Butter 2 half 13 x 18-inch (33 x 45-cm) sheet
pans and line with parchment paper.

Make the cake batter in a medium-sized
bowl. Sift together the flour, baking powder, and salt.

In the bowl of a stand mixer fitted with
the whisk attachment, whip the eggs until tripled in volume. Add the granulated
sugar and whip for 3 minutes. With the
mixer on medium speed, add the melted and cooled butter in a steady stream.
Add the vanilla, orange zest, and 1 tablespoon of the clementine marmalade. Add
the flour mixture and whip until just
combined. Spread the batter evenly on
the prepared baking sheets and bake for
about 15 minutes, or until lightly golden
around the edges.

Arrange 2 clean dishcloths on a work
surface and sprinkle all over with confectioners' sugar. Invert each cake onto a
towel and sprinkle with more confectioners' sugar. Starting on the shorter ends,
roll up each cake into a log shape, then
let cool to almost room temperature.

Unroll each cake and spread a layer of
clementine marmalade on top of each.
Spread a thin layer of white chocolate
ganache on top of the marmalade. Cut each
cake lengthwise in half, then roll up each
piece to form 4 logs. Arrange the 4 logs
end-to-end to form 1 extra-long log, which
will be your final cake. Arrange the log
vertically on a cake board or serving plate
and cover with the remaining ganache. If
the ganache is too firm, gently warm it in a
microwave or over a bain-marie until it is
a spreadable consistency.

Decorate as you like best.

Torta Di Natale
E Compleanno Per Charis

CHRISTMAS BIRTHDAY CAKE FOR CHARIS

Ingredients

12 servings

For the cake
- *2 ⅓ cups (300g)* all-purpose flour, sifted
- *1 cup (100g)* organic potato starch
- *2 tablespoons* baking powder
- *4 large* organic eggs
- *1 ¼ (260g)* sugar
- *2 teaspoons* vanilla bean paste or pure vanilla extract
- *1 ½ cups (400ml)* double whipping cream

For the milk chocolate ganache
- *17.6 ounces (500g)* milk chocolate chips or finely chopped milk chocolate
- *2 ¼ cups (500ml)* double whipping cream

For the Swiss meringue buttercream
- *8 large* organic egg whites
- *2 ½ cups (500g)* sugar
- *¼ teaspoon* salt
- *1 teaspoon* vanilla bean paste or pure vanilla extract
- *3 cups (680g)* unsalted butter, at room temperature and cut into cubes

For the meringue topping
- *4 large* organic egg whites
- *½ cup (100g)* sugar
- *½ teaspoon* cream of tartar
- *1 teaspoon* vanilla bean paste or pure vanilla extract

To decorate
- Vegan Marshmallows (see recipe at page 106)

*T*his cake is dedicated to my dear friend, Charis, who was born the day after Christmas, as well as to anyone born during the holiday season. It's one more reason to celebrate, and another excuse to bake a delicious cake. Obviously, you can prepare this cake whenever you wish, but it works very well as a celebration cake to display as a centerpiece on festive tables. So, I dedicate this recipe to Charis, who has been my friend for many years now, and to all of you, whose birthdays are a little over-shadowed by the frenetic holiday celebrations. The moment it stands on your table will be your special moment!

Method

Preheat the oven to 350°F (180°C). Butter 2 8-inch (20-cm) round cake pans and line the bottoms with parchment paper.

Make the cake batter in a large bowl. Sift together the flour, potato starch, and baking powder.

In the bowl of a stand mixer fitted with the whisk attachment or using a hand-held mixer, combine the eggs, sugar, and vanilla and whip until doubled in volume and pale in color.

In a large-sized bowl, use a hand-held mixer to whip the cream until stiff peaks form.

Add the flour mixture to the egg mixture and gently fold to combine, then add the whipped cream and gently fold to combine. Divide the batter between the prepared pans and bake for 40 to 45 minutes, or until a wooden toothpick inserted in the center of the cakes comes out clean. Let the cakes cool in the pans for 15 minutes, then invert onto a wire rack to cool completely.

Make the milk chocolate ganache by placing the chocolate in a heat-proof bowl. In a small saucepan, bring the cream to a gentle boil, then pour it over the chocolate, let stand for 30 seconds, and then whisk until smooth and glossy. Let cool at room temperature until ready to use.

Make the Swiss meringue buttercream in a metal bowl set over a pan of simmering water. Combine the egg whites, sugar, and salt, whisking constantly until the sugar is fully dissolved and the mixture reaches 160°F (71°C).

Transfer to the bowl of a stand mixer fitted with the whisk attachment and whip on medium-high for about 10 minutes, or

→

until the bowl is cool to the touch and egg whites are stiff. Add the vanilla and whip to incorporate. Switch to the paddle attachment and with the mixer on low, start adding the butter. Continue beating until the buttercream is creamy and shiny. Refrigerate the buttercream and allow it to set while you prepare the cake.

To assemble, you can create a one-layer-filled cake by joining the two cakes together, or you can slice through to each layer and achieve a three-layer-filled cake. If you wish to go for this option, now is the time to do it. Once you have sliced your cake, place 1 layer on a cake board or serving plate. Fill a piping bag with some Swiss meringue buttercream and pipe a circle around the edge of the cake to prevent the ganache from dripping. Repeat for each layer (if you choose to cut more layers). Then fill each center with the ganache, reserving 200g or 250g for the decoration. Place the second layer on top of the first, then cover the top and sides of the cake with a thin layer of the buttercream to create a crumb coat. Refrigerate the cake to firm up the buttercream, then cover the top and sides with the remaining buttercream. Refrigerate the cake while you make the meringue topping.

Make the meringue topping in a metal bowl set over a pan of simmering water. Combine the egg whites, sugar, and cream of tartar, whisking constantly until the sugar is fully dissolved and the mixture reaches 160°F (71°C). Transfer to the bowl of a stand mixer fitted with the whisk attachment and whip on medium-high for about 10 minutes, or until the bowl is cool to the touch and egg whites are stiff. Add the vanilla and whip to incorporate.

If the leftover ganache is too firm, warm it slightly in the microwave until it reaches a pouring consistency, but isn't so warm that it will melt the buttercream. Using a spoon, drip some of the ganache around the edges of the cake, allowing it drip down the sides, then fill the center with more ganache. Allow the ganache to firm up at room temperature.

Fill a piping bag fitted with an open star tip with the marshmallow topping and pipe rosettes or other motifs of your choice on top of the cake, then carefully toast them with a blowtorch. Decorate with vegan marshmallows, toasting if desired, and any additional decorations you wish and serve. Happy Birthday!

Baked Alaska My Way

"*Baby, it's cold outside,*" as the famous song says. But I say, it's warm inside, so making this frozen cake will bring a welcome freshness after the comfort of a festive meal. Plus, talk about a showstopper! Baked Alaska is the queen of all showstoppers! This version has been simplified to help you save some time in the kitchen and focus on what is most important—being together with the people you love! The only thing you need is a little patience. Each step requires chilling time in the freezer, but the rest is very easy. You can also make the ice cream base days ahead and spread the meringue right before serving time.*

Note: You will need an 8-cup (2-liter) metal bowl or another freezer-safe container. Traditionally, Baked Alaska is made in a dome-shaped bowl, but you can play with other shapes, too. Also, you can change the ice cream flavors and experiment with countless combinations! You will also need a blowtorch, which I find to be the best way to brown the meringue. Fun, fun, fun!

Ingredients

8 servings

- *32 ounces (800g)* chocolate ice cream
- *24 ounces (600g)* stracciatella ice cream
- *24 ounces (600g)* pistachio ice cream
- *4* large organic egg whites, at room temperature
- *½ cup (100g)* sugar
- *1 teaspoon* vanilla bean paste or the seeds from *1* vanilla bean

Method

Line an 8-cup (2-liter) dome-shaped metal bowl or another freezer-safe container with plastic wrap, leaving about 1.5 inches (4 cm) hanging off the sides. Spread the chocolate ice cream all the way up the sides of the bowl, trying to create an even layer. You will end up with a cavity in the middle. Place the bowl in the freezer for 20 minutes or until hard. Repeat with the stracciatella ice cream, followed by the pistachio ice cream, returning the bowl to the freezer for 20 minutes between each layer. Use the over-hanging plastic wrap to tightly cover the ice cream, then freeze for at least 4 hours, but preferably overnight.

When you are ready to serve the cake, place your cake stand or serving plate in the freezer while you make the meringue.

In the bowl of a stand mixer fitted with the whisk attachment or using a hand-held mixer, beat the egg whites on high speed until frothy. Gradually add the sugar in small portions, then add the vanilla and beat on high speed until stiff peaks form. Working quickly, remove the bowl from the freezer, unwrap the plastic wrap from the top, and pull on it to loosen the ice cream. Arrange your cake stand or serving plate on top of the ice cream and carefully flip it over, then remove the bowl and the plastic wrap. Using the back of a spoon, spread the meringue all over the ice cream, creating waves or other patterns as desired. Working quickly and carefully, use a blowtorch to brown the meringue until it looks toasted but not burnt. Serve right away.

Chocolate Stout Beer Cake

Ingredients

12 slices

For the cake
- *2 cups* plus *2 tablespoons (275g)* all-purpose flour, sifted
- *2 ½ teaspoons* baking soda
- *¼ teaspoon* salt
- *1 ⅓ cups (300g)* unsalted butter
- *1 ¼ cups (300ml)* stout beer, at room temperature
- *2 cups (400g)* granulated sugar
- *4 ounces (100g)* good quality dark chocolate, melted
- *⅞ cup (90g)* unsweetened cocoa powder
- *½ cup* plus *2 tablespoons (150ml)* sour cream
- *3 large* organic eggs
- *1 ½ teaspoons* vanilla bean paste or pure vanilla extract

For the cream cheese frosting
- *1 cup* plus *2 tablespoons (250g)* unsalted butter, at room temperature
- *2 cups* plus *3 tablespoons (500g)* cream cheese
- *1 ¾ cups (180 g)* confectioners' sugar, sifted
- *1 teaspoon* vanilla bean paste or pure vanilla extract
- Poppy seeds, to decorate

*T*hank you, Ireland, for this recipe!! Though this cake is traditionally made for St. Patrick's Day, I bake it every time I feel in need of something decadent with a complex and aromatic taste. In this cake, you have it all. Velvety chocolate mixes with the complex flavor of stout beer, and when these two ingredients come together they release the most incredible aroma. Last but not least, fresh and tangy cream cheese frosting is the perfect topping. I first heard about this cake from a London flatmate, who was Irish and talked very highly of this traditional dessert. Of course, I had to go in search of it, and after much reading on the subject, I came up with my own adapted version. I think cake and booze are a match made in heaven, especially during the holidays.

Method

Preheat the oven to 350°F (175°C) and butter and flour 2 8-inch (20 cm) round cake pans.

In a large bowl, combine the flour, baking soda, and salt.

In a microwave-safe, medium-sized bowl, combine the butter and beer and micro-wave until fully melted. Add the granulated sugar, chocolate, and cocoa powder and stir to combine.

In a large bowl, whisk together the sour cream and eggs. Add the vanilla, followed by the beer mixture, and whisk until fully incorporated. Add the flour mixture and stir. Pour the batter into the prepared pans and bake for 45 to 50 minutes, or until a toothpick inserted in the centers come out clean. Let cool in the pans, then invert the cakes onto a serving plate.

Make the cream cheese frosting in the bowl of a stand mixer fitted with the paddle attachment, and beat the butter until there are no lumps. Then add the cream cheese and beat for about 4 minutes or until creamy. Add the confectioners' sugar and beat until fully combined and smooth. Add the vanilla and beat to incorporate.

Place 1 cake layer on a cake stand or serving plate and spread with a layer of cream cheese frosting. Place the second cake layer on top of the frosting, then spread another layer of cream cheese frosting over the top. Sprinkle with poppy seeds to decorate (if desired), and serve.

Trifle Al Cioccolato E Arancia
CHOCOLATE-ORANGE TRIFLE

Ingredients

About 8 servings

For the orange-vanilla syrup
- *1 ½ cups (300g)* sugar
- *3 tablespoons* orange-flavored liqueur, such as Grand Marnier
- *1 teaspoon* vanilla bean paste or pure vanilla extract

For the orange loaf cake
- *2 ⅓ cups plus 2 tablespoons plus 2 teaspoons (320g)* all-purpose flour
- *1 ½ teaspoons* baking powder
- *6 large organic eggs*
- *1 ½ cups plus 1 ½ tablespoons (320g)* sugar
- *1 ⅓ cups (300g)* unsalted butter, melted
- Freshly-grated zest and freshly-squeezed juice of *2 large organic oranges*
- *2 teaspoons* vanilla bean paste or pure vanilla extract
- *2 ¼ cups (730g)* good quality orange marmalade

For the chocolate custard
- *2 ¼ ounces (60g)* dark chocolate, chopped
- *2 ¼ ounces (60g)* semisweet chocolate, chopped
- *3 cups (720ml)* whole milk
- *⅔ cup plus 2 teaspoons (160ml)* double whipping cream
- *3 large organic eggs*
- *½ cup (100g)* sugar
- *½ cup (60g)* organic cornstarch

To assemble
- *10 ounces (250g)* amaretti cookies (optional)
- *1 cup plus 2 teaspoons (250ml)* double whipping cream
- *4 ¾ ounces (120g)* chocolate shavings or chips

If you, like me, are a fan of "Friends," you probably remember the English trifle Rachel made on a Thanksgiving episode. Well, having mincemeat inside is definately not how a trifle should be made! LOL! This isn't a traditional English trifle either, but it's a decadent one. Trifle, to me, calls for celebration, so what better time of the year than Christmas to make it?!

Method

Make the orange-vanilla syrup in a medium-sized saucepan. Combine the sugar and 1 ¼ cups (300 ml) of water over medium heat and cook until the sugar is completely dissolved and the liquid comes to a gentle boil. Remove from the heat, add the orange-flavored liqueur and vanilla, and stir to incorporate. Let cool at room temperature.

Preheat the oven to 350°F (180°C). Butter a 16-ounce (400-g) loaf pan and line with parchment paper.

Make the cake batter in a large bowl. Sift together the flour and baking powder.

In the bowl of a stand mixer fitted with the whisk attachment or using a hand-held mixer, whip the eggs and sugar until very pale. Add the melted butter and stir gently to combine without deflating the mixture. Add the orange zest and juice and the vanilla and gently mix to combine. Add the flour mixture and gently fold to combine, scraping the bottom of the bowl as needed to incorporate all of the flour. Pour into the prepared loaf pan and bake for 40 to 45 minutes, or until a toothpick inserted in the center comes out clean. Let the loaf cool completely in the pan on a wire rack, then cut into slices. Arrange the slices on a tray and pour or brush on the orange-vanilla syrup until they are soaked. Spread a generous amount of orange marmalade on each slice.

Make the chocolate custard and place both chocolates in a medium-sized bowl. In a large saucepan, bring the milk and cream to a gentle simmer. In a separate bowl, whisk together the eggs, sugar, and cornstarch until there are no lumps. Gradually add the hot milk mixture, stirring constantly. Pour the custard into the saucepan and cook over low-medium heat, stirring constantly, until thick.

Pour over the chocolate and stir until completely melted. Pass the custard through a sieve, cover in plastic wrap, and refrigerate to set for at least 2 hours and preferably overnight.

Assemble the trifle by arranging a layer of cake slices in the form of fingers in the bottom of a 10-cup (2.5-liter) glass trifle dish, then top with a layer of chocolate custard and sprinkle with some crushed amaretti cookies (if desired). Repeat to add more layers. You can stop at 2 layers, but I recommend filling the dish to the top for a more impressive result. Refrigerate for a couple of hours, or overnight if the trifle is made ahead of time.

Whip the cream to medium-soft peaks, then spread on top of the trifle. Decorate with chocolate shavings and more amaretti cookies and serve.

Biancomangiare all'Amaretto

Ingredients

Serves 6–8, depending on the size and shape of the mold

- *1 cup (180g)* sugar
- *⅔ cup (85g)* organic cornstarch
- *4 cups (1 liter)* whole milk
- *1 teaspoon* vanilla bean paste or pure vanilla extract
- *1 tablespoon* amaretto

I've always been a big fan of pudding. Chocolate pudding, vanilla pudding, panna cotta, pudding made in individual cups, pudding made in gorgeous bundt cake molds. You name it and I have had it or made it and I will not stop. For as long as I live, there will be pudding!

This is an especially attractive pudding, thanks to the mold I use, which is a replica of a Victorian jelly mold, but it's also a very special recipe. Biancomangiare dates back to medieval times. Although it was brought here from the Middle East, today Italians claim ownership of the original recipe. France has its own version, called Blanc-Manger, while Spain has one, too. It's very popular in Sicily, but also in Val D'Aosta and the area around Naples. This version is flavored with amaretto, but each place makes Biancomangiare using its own local products like almonds, honey, cinnamon, or even lemon! It doesn't matter who made it first. What's important is that Biancomangiare can be enjoyed by all. And now, I wish for you to share it at your Christmas table. It's light and slightly aromatic and it looks like white snow! Kids love it and adults crave it!

Method

In a medium-sized saucepan set over medium heat, combine the sugar and cornstarch. Gradually add the milk, whisking to prevent lumps. Keep at a gentle boil for about 3 minutes, stirring constantly, or until thickened. Remove from the heat, then add the vanilla and amaretto. Run a medium-sized mold or individual cups (such as 6 standard ramekins) under cold water and do not dry—this will make it easier to release the pudding later.

Pour the hot pudding mixture into the mold or cups and let cool at room temperature until it is solid. Refrigerate for at least 3 hours. This can be made one or two days ahead and kept in the fridge. To serve, invert the mold on to a serving plate and portion it using a spoon.

Small
TREATS
Other Bakes
& More

Ricciarelli Di Siena

ALMOND COOKIES FROM SIENA

These delicious cookies are all about history, and the Tuscan city of Siena has quite a colorful past. Ricciarelli cookies used to be prepared in convents by nuns or in what we now call pharmacies—two places where spices were easy to find. The story behind these cookies is that a soldier named Ricciardetto della Gherardesca brought some new and special Arab cookies to Italy. They became what we know today as ricciarelli. In Italy, they are a must at the very end of a meal, after all of the other cakes are served, and they are usually paired with a glass of Moscato wine or a sweet liqueur.

Ingredients

Makes 30 to 40 cookies

For the syrup
- ½ cup (100g) sugar

For the cookies
- 16 ounces (400g) whole unpeeled almonds
- 1 ⅓ cups (270g) sugar
- Grated zest of 1 large organic orange
- ¼ cup (30g) all-purpose flour
- ½ teaspoon almond oil or pure almond extract
- 2 large organic egg whites
- Confectioners' sugar for dusting
- 3 to 4 sheets wafer paper (if you can't find this, don't worry, the cookies will still be delicious)

Method

Make the syrup in a small saucepan over medium heat. Bring the sugar and 2 tablespoons plus 2 teaspoons (40 ml) of water to a boil without stirring. Let cool slightly.

Make the cookies in a food processor by combining the almonds, 1 cup plus 3 tablespoons (240 g) of the sugar, and the orange peel, and pulse until it has a superfine texture similar to almond flour. Transfer to a large bowl, then add the flour and stir until fully combined.

Add the almond oil, followed by the warm but not too hot syrup, and mix by hand. Keep mixing until combined. Cover with plastic wrap and let rest at room temperature for at least 12 hours and preferably overnight.

Using a hand-held mixer, whip the egg whites and the remaining 2 tablespoons plus 1 teaspoon (30 g) of sugar until frothy. Add the egg white mixture to the rested dough, and mix by hand until compact and firm. If the dough sticks to your hands, add a little confectioners' sugar. Using your hands, shape the dough into a log, wrap in plastic wrap, and refrigerate until ready to use.

Using a medium-sized oval cookie cutter or an oval paper template, trace 30 to 40 oval shapes onto the wafer paper, then use scissors to cut out the ovals.

Preheat the oven to 350°F (175°C) and line a baking sheet with parchment paper.

Using your hands, shape the dough into a long cylinder about 2 inches (5 cm) in diameter. Spread the confectioners' sugar on a plate or board and roll the cylinder of dough through the sugar. Next, cut the cylinder crosswise into ½-inch (1.25-cm) thick slices. Shape each slice into an oval the same size and shape as the wafer paper ovals.

Arrange the wafer paper ovals on the parchment-lined baking sheet, then place each oval cookie on a piece of wafer paper, gently pressing down to slightly flatten the shape. Dust with plenty of confectioners' sugar and bake for about 10 minutes, or until lightly golden around the edges, but still pale in the center. Let cool completely on the baking sheet.

Holiday Steamed Pudding

"Hallo! A great deal of steam! The pudding was out of the copper. A smell like a washing-day! That was the cloth. A smell like an eating-house and a pastry cook's next door to each other, with a laundress's next door to that! That was the pudding! In half a minute Mrs. Cratchit entered—flushed, but smiling proudly—with the pudding, like a speckled cannon-ball, so hard and firm, blazing in half of half-a-quartern of ignited brandy, and bedight with Christmas holly stuck into the top." Charles Dickens, "A Christmas Carol"

Who hasn't heard of Charles Dickens and his beloved classic, "A Christmas Carol"? This book has accompanied me since early childhood. I think I have read it at least four times, watched the film even more. Still, every year, Dickens' vision and his description of the holidays immediately put me in the mood to bake! This is not the traditional English figgy pudding, but it is a steamed pudding, and definitely a quicker one to make. At Christmas, this pudding is the "pièce de résistance" of a true holiday meal!

Ingredients

6/8 servings

- ⅓ cup plus *1 teaspoon (80ml)* light cream
- Freshly-squeezed juice of *1* organic lemon
- *2 ½ cups* plus *2 teaspoons (330g)* all-purpose flour, sifted
- *2 teaspoons* baking powder
- *1 ½ cups (350g)* unsalted butter, at room temperature
- *1 ¾ cups (350g)* sugar
- *2 teaspoons* vanilla bean paste, pure vanilla extract, or a vanilla pod
- Freshly-grated zest of *1* large organic orange
- *4* large organic eggs

For the port-poached pears
- *3 cups (720ml)* Ruby Port
- *1 cup (200g)* sugar
- *2 sticks* cinnamon
- *3 cloves*
- *2 star anise*
- *2 teaspoons* vanilla bean paste, pure vanilla extract, or a vanilla pod
- The peel of *1* large organic orange
- *3 Bosc (Kaiser) pears*

Method

Preheat the oven to 350°F (180°C) and bring a kettle of water to a boil. Butter and flour a lidded 8-cup (2-liter) steamed pudding mold. In a small glass bowl, combine the cream and lemon juice. Stir, cover, and let stand at room temperature until ready to use; the cream will curdle.

Sift the flour and baking powder into a large bowl.

In the bowl of a stand mixer fitted with the paddle attachment, combine the butter, sugar, vanilla, and orange zest. Beat on medium-high speed until light and fluffy—the mixture will smell sublime! Scrape down the sides of the bowl and with the mixer on medium speed, add the eggs 1 at a time, beating until fully combined. Add the sifted flour mixture in three portions, then add the curdled cream. Using a spatula, give the batter a final stir then pour it into the pudding mold. Cover and seal the mold, then place it on the dishcloth inside the larger pan—this will ensure the pudding doesn't move around while in the oven. Pour enough boiling water into the larger pan to go halfway up the sides of the mold and bake for about 2 hours (or more, depending on the oven). When the baking time is almost over, carefully remove the lid of the mold and test to see if it is done by inserting a wooden toothpick in the center of the pudding to see if it comes out clean. Carefully remove both pans from the oven, but leave the mold in the larger pan until the water is cool. Remove the lid of the mold and invert it on a serving plate or stand.

While the pudding is baking, poach the pears.

In a large saucepan, combine the port, sugar, cinnamon, cloves, star anise, vanilla, and orange peel.

Peel the pears and cut the bottoms slightly to remove the cores; leave the stems attached.

Place the saucepan over medium heat, add the pears and bring to a simmer. Cook for about 15 minutes or until soft, but not overcooked. Let stand in the poaching liquid until completely cool. Transfer the pears to a plate and strain the poaching liquid to remove the orange peel and spices. Return the poaching liquid to the saucepan, place over medium heat and bring to a boil. Lower the heat and simmer for about 15 minutes, or until reduced to a thick syrup. Cut the pears in half, arrange them on top of the steamed pudding, and drizzle with the warm port reduction. Serve immediately.

Praline Al Mascarpone

Ingredients

Makes about 40 pralines

- *16 ounces (400g)* good quality dark chocolate, finely chopped
- *8 ounces (200g)* firm mascarpone cheese
- *½ teaspoon liqueur (optional)*

To decorate
- *1 ounce (25g)* unsweetened cocoa powder
- *2 ¾ ounces (70g)* shredded coconut
- *2 ounces (50g)* pistachios, crushed
- *1 ½ ounces (40g)* hazelnuts, crushed

Want to be the queen or king of your Christmas or New Year's Eve parties? The person your guests will congratulate? Look no further and make my Mascarpone Pralines! They are the easiest and yet most delicious little treats around. Plus, the flavor options are endless and so are the decorations. Make them more festive by rolling them in edible glitters, pearl sugar, or edible rainbow dust. I like to keep them pretty, but also rustic looking. And I love different textures, so besides edible glitter that provides a little sparkle, I use crushed pistachios, coconut rapè (shredded coconut), cocoa powder, and chocolate ganache. Mix in ½ teaspoon of your favourite liquor if you want. Chambord, a raspberry liqueur, is probably my favorite, but feel free to play with whatever you like! Kids will love rolling the pralines with you! It's another great excuse to be together during the holidays.

Method

In a bain-marie or a metal bowl set over a pan of simmering water, melt the dark chocolate, stirring occasionally.

While the chocolate is melting, remove the mascarpone from the refrigerator and give it a quick stir.

Once the chocolate is fully melted, let cool until just warm to the touch, then fold in the mascarpone. If you choose to flavor your pralines with liqueur, stir it in now. If you want to use more than 1 liqueur, divide the chocolate mixture in equal parts and add the liqueurs in equal portions. Cover with plastic wrap and refrigerate for about 2 ½ hours or until set.

Once the chocolate is set, use wet hands to roll it into balls, roughly ½ ounce (12.5g) each.

Pour the cocoa powder, coconut, pistachios, and hazelnuts into separate bowls. Roll each praline in 1 of the decorations and lay in a small paper petit fours cup for serving. If you want to make the pralines ahead, wait to roll them in the decorations and store them without toppings in the refrigerator overnight. Roll the pralines in the decorations just before serving, so the toppings remain crunchy. I like to serve them in a large Sheffield or silver tray and pass them around during the party—they fly off the tray in a matter of minutes!

Biscotti Allo Zenzero
GINGER COOKIES

*T*hese cookies are nothing like the gingerbread cookies we all know. They have a buttery and crumbly texture and I find them delicious. I am not a super fan of gingerbread cookies, but these ones remind me more of a shortbread kind of cookie with a lovely gingery spicy flavor. Allow the cookies to fully cool down before lifting them up because they can break easily.

Ingredients

About 20 medium-sized cookies

- *2 tablespoons* freshly-grated ginger
- *¾ cup* plus *1 teaspoon (175g)* unsalted butter, at room temperature
- *¼ cup* plus *2 teaspoons (60g)* brown sugar
- *2 teaspoons* vanilla bean paste or pure vanilla extract
- *2 large* organic egg yolks
- *2 ⅓ cups (300g)* all-purpose flour
- *2 ½ teaspoons* ground ginger
- *1 teaspoon* ground cinnamon
- *¼ teaspoon* ground nutmeg
- *3 whole* cloves, crushed

Method

In a small bowl, combine the freshly-grated ginger with 3 tablespoons of water. Chill in the refrigerator for about 30 minutes or until very cold. Pour the water through a small sieve and set aside; discard the ginger.

In the bowl of a stand mixer fitted with the paddle attachment, beat the butter and brown sugar on medium speed until light and fluffy. Add the vanilla, then add the egg yolks, one at a time, beating after each addition.

In a medium-sized bowl, whisk together the flour, ground ginger, cinnamon, nutmeg, and crushed cloves.

With the stand mixer on low, gradually add the flour mixture, mixing until fully incorporated. Gradually add the cold ginger-infused water and mix until just incorporated.

On a lightly-floured work surface, use a rolling pin to roll out the dough until about 1/8-inch thick (4 mm). Cover in plastic wrap and transfer to a baking sheet, then let it chill in the refrigerator for at least 4 hours and preferably overnight.

Preheat the oven to 350°F (180°C) and line a baking sheet with parchment paper.

Cut the dough into the desired shapes and arrange on the prepared baking sheet. Bake for 10 to 12 minutes (depending on the size of your cookies) or until slightly golden.

Cookies can be made ahead and stored in an airtight container for up to 5 days.

Addormenta Suocere

ALMOND PRALINES

*A*ttention!!!! This is a highly addictive recipe! I am sure that each and every one of you around the world has tried, at least once, (perhaps at a Christmas fair), this incredibly delicious and yet very simple treat. I know I have, and I also know I love these almond pralines today as much as I loved them when I was a child. In Italian they are called "Addormenta suocere," which translates to something like "the sleepy mother-in-law" or even better "to make mothers-in-law fall asleep." Typically, these beloved sweets, originally from the regions of Tuscany and Umbria, are sucked until they melt in your mouth and never chewed. They used to be offered to mothers-in-law to keep them quiet—they'd be so busy melting the almonds in their mouths that they would stay silent until they fell asleep. Oh, how I love traditions and legends like these!

The smell of almond pralines is simply outstanding and brings back childhood memories of toys, music, and fun times at Christmas. They also have a divine texture and make a sweet gift if wrapped in a paper bag. I love to present them as a wonderful surprise at the end of a meal, when all the guests are gathered around the table enjoying every minute of it. Once you serve these pralines, I know they'll be the talk of the evening!

Method

Line a large baking sheet with parchment paper.

Place the almonds, sugar, and ½ cup plus 1 tablespoon (135ml) of water in a medium-sized saucepan (avoid using nonstick, as the sugar won't caramelize properly) over medium heat. Stir often for about 3 minutes, never leaving the pan unattended, or until the almonds are fully coated and start to turn a beautiful amber color. Carefully spread the almonds in an even layer on the prepared baking sheet and let cool completely before serving.

Ingredients

5 small bags to give as a present to serve about 5 people

- *24 ounces (600g)* blanched whole almonds
- *2 ½ cups (500g)* sugar
- *½ cup* plus *1 tablespoon (140ml)* water

Florentines

LACE COOKIES

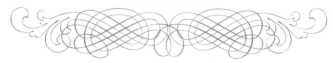

Ingredients

About 12 medium
or 24 small cookies

- *2 tablespoons (30g)*
  unsalted butter
- *2 tablespoons (30g)*
  brown sugar
- *2 tablespoons (15g)*
  all-purpose flour
- *1 ¼ ounces (30g) clear*
  liquid honey

I've included this recipe because of how fun it is to decorate. After all, Christmas is about decoration, whether you're decorating your house, your table, or adding a nice bow to your Christmas presents. It is about creating the atmosphere around us, so this recipe has been developed to give you a super simple and quick way to add an extra touch to your creations. We must thank Catherine De Medici, the Italian noblewoman who ruled France until 1563. She was what we would call "a modern woman" for her time, and to this day, we still enjoy many of the recipes she brought from France to Italy and vice versa. Florentines are one such recipe.

When still warm but cool to the touch, you can mold these lace cookies in almost any shape you like and use them however you please. Place them on a plate to create a base where you can lay a dollop of ice cream, or simply put them on your favorite cake. Don't be scared of the small quantities of the ingredients—you can double, triple, or even quadruple the recipe as you please. And finally, you can serve them at

the end of your lunch or dinner, with a glass of Vin Santo wine. It will be the perfect ending to a perfect Christmas meal!

Method

Preheat the oven to 350°F (180°C) and line a baking sheet with parchment paper or a silicone baking mat.

In a small saucepan over low heat, combine the butter, brown sugar, flour, and honey and warm until everything melts together. Let it cool for 10 minutes maximum. Carefully transfer to a pastry bag or icing bottle and pipe 1-inch (3-cm) large dots on the parchment-lined baking sheet, leaving 2 inches (5 cm) between each dot. Bake for 8 minutes or until golden. Let cool briefly, but while the cookies are still warm, lift them up and bend them to create your desired shape. You can also leave them round and flat and serve them with a bowl of ice cream or pudding.

Vegan Marshmallows

When people ask me about my work, I always say that I do not use animal gelatin, artificial colorants, additives, or preservatives in my recipes. I am a vegetarian, and as I've said many times before, if I can't eat it, I will not sell it! So, it took me a long time to figure out how to achieve the best structure, consistency, and appearance for some of my recipes, including marshmallows. Thankfully, we have many options and substitutes available. So, here is a super simple recipe, using aquafaba, which is nothing more than the leftover water from a can of chickpeas! And because marshmallows are a must during Christmas, I had to add this recipe to my book. I simply had to! Marshmallows make a lovely present for friends. They can be colored with 100 percent natural edible pigments or dried fruit powders, and they can be flavored by adding cocoa powder or coffee granules, just to name a few options. Save some marshmallows to decorate the Torta di Natale e Compleanno per Charis (page 68).

Ingredients

About 80 marshmallows

- *1 cup* plus *2 teaspoons (250ml)* aquafaba (the liquid from 2 cans of chickpeas)
- *½ teaspoon* cream of tartar
- *3 teaspoons* vanilla bean paste or pure vanilla extract
- *2 tablespoons* agar agar powder
- *1 ½ cups* plus *2 tablespoons (160g)* confectioners' sugar, plus more for dusting and tossing

Method

Generously dust 2 8-inch (20-cm) square baking pans with icing sugar.

In the bowl of a stand mixer fitted with the whisk attachment, combine the aquafaba and cream of tartar and whip until fluffy. Add the vanilla and whip for about 10 minutes or until stiff peaks form.

In a medium saucepan, combine the agar powder and 2 cups plus 1 tablespoon plus 1 teaspoon (500 ml) of water and bring to a boil. Continue boiling, stirring constantly, for about 3 minutes. Add the confectioners' sugar, stirring constantly (to avoid burning), for 4 minutes or until dense.

With the mixer on low, add the hot sugar syrup to the aquafaba in a slow, steady stream and beat for about 35 seconds. Pour into the prepared pans and generously dust with confectioners' sugar. Let cool at room temperature for at least 1 hour.

Preheat the oven to 275°F (130°C) and line a baking sheet with parchment paper.

Cut the cooled marshmallows into squares or any shape you like and toss in more confectioners' sugar. Turn the oven off. Arrange the marshmallows on the parchment-lined baking sheet and let dry in the warm oven for 1 hour.

Calissons

Ingredients

About 40 Calissons

For the Calissons
- *10 ounces (250g)* candied melon
- *1 ½ ounces (40g)* candied orange peel
- *1 ¼ ounces (30g)* candied lemon peel
- *2 cups (200g)* confectioners' sugar
- *2 ¾ cups (300g)* almond flour
- *2 tablespoons* orange blossom water
- *1 tablespoon* apricot jam, strained to remove any chunks
- *2 sheets* wafer paper, size A4 or more (depending of the size of cutter)

For the royal icing
- *1 ¾ cups (175g)* confectioners' sugar
- *1* large organic egg white

The holidays are a time to indulge, and though I rarely need an excuse, for some reason around this time of year, I feel even more inclined to enjoy whatever my body and spirit crave. Calissons are little French treats made with almond flour, which gives them a marzipan-like texture. They are simply delicious, especially served at the end of a meal with a glass of sweet wine, and surrounded by laughter and joy! If you have an old vintage box, fill it with Calissons and wrap a nice velvet ribbon around for the perfect gift!

Method

In a food processor, combine the candied melon, orange peel, and lemon peel and blitz until a fine paste forms. Transfer to the bowl of a stand mixer fitted with the paddle attachment. Add the confectioners' sugar and beat until incorporated, then add the almond flour and beat until combined. Add the orange blossom water and beat until fully mixed.

Arrange a sheet of parchment paper on a work surface and line a baking sheet with a sheet of wafer paper. Brush a very thin layer of apricot jam over the wafer paper. On the parchment paper, use a rolling pin to roll the dough until about 1/2-inch thick (1.25 cm), then lift it and place it over the wafer paper, making sure it sticks properly. Brush with another very thin layer of apricot jam and top with a second sheet of wafer paper.

Using a Calisson cutter, cut the dough into oval shapes, stopping to clean the cutter every 2 or 3 cuts.

Let rest for 5 minutes.

Make the royal icing in a large bowl by whisking together the confectioners' sugar and egg white until liquid, but not too runny, and lump free.

Using a small offset spatula or piping bag, spread the royal icing over each Calisson, following the shape, and cleaning the sides as you go to avoid dripping. Arrange the Calissons on a serving plate or silver tray for serving, or wrap them as Christmas gifts for those you love! Stored in an airtight container, they will keep for up to one week.

ra Duse
o intorno al mondo

Decadent Chocolate Squares

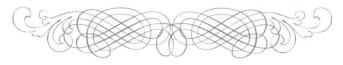

Ingredients

About 25 squares

- *8 ounces (200g)* good quality dark chocolate, finely chopped
- *5 ½ ounces (140g)* good quality milk chocolate, finely chopped
- *1 cup (225ml)* heavy cream
- *1 teaspoon* hazelnut liqueur, such as Frangelico, or another liqueur of your choice
- *1 tablespoon (15g)* unsalted butter
- Unsweetened cocoa powder, for decorating

*C*hristmas is all about preparation, from making food and wrapping presents to decorating the house and planning the many gatherings the holidays require. When in need of a simple, quick, and amazingly delicious treat, this recipe is just what you need. These squares can be wrapped or boxed and given away as edible presents for friends or work colleagues, but they look triumphant displayed on a cake stand, sprinkled with edible glitter for a super festive look! If you do give them away as presents, keep in mind that they are made with fresh cream, so their shelf life isn't long and they are best stored in the fridge. You can add ingredients of your choice to make them even more special!

Method

Line an 8-inch (20-cm) square baking dish with parchment paper, pressing against the sides and bottom to make sure the parchment adheres completely without any wrinkles.

In a medium-sized saucepan over medium-low heat, bring the heavy cream to a gentle simmer. As soon as the first bubbles start to appear, remove from the heat. Add the dark and milk chocolates, let rest for 1 minute, and then use a spatula to gently stir until the chocolate is fully melted. Add the butter. Use a whisk to give the mixture a final stir, being careful not to lift the whisk or you will create air bubbles. Add the liqueur and stir until combined. Pour the mixture into the parchment-lined baking dish and freeze for at least 4 hours and preferably overnight.

When ready to serve, invert the pan onto a sheet of parchment paper set on the counter and lift up the pan to release the chocolate. Fill a jug with boiling water. Insert a long paring knife into the hot water and leave it to warm for a little while. Dry the blade and start cutting the chocolate into bars. Continue cutting, warming the knife in the water and drying it as needed to ensure sharp and clean cuts.

In a large bowl, toss the squares in some cocoa powder until they are coated. Let set on the counter for a few minutes, then serve or wrap in your chosen box or bag if you wish to offer them as presents.

Springerle Cookies

The Italian baker baking a German classic! First, let me pay my most humble respect to German baking. Second, let me say that I never consider my recipes to be better than the originals. After searching many German recipe books on the subject, I have come up with this simple version. I simply love Springerle cookies, so I include them on my list of all-time favorite holiday recipes. You can find traditional Springerle molds online, or if you find yourself in any German city during Christmas, head straight to one of their beautiful Christmas markets and stock up on cookie molds. If you can't find a mold, you can use the bottom of an antique water glass to impress patterns on your dough. Traditionally, antique water glasses used to have pretty patterns imprinted on the bottom. Ask your Grandma, she will tell you!

Ingredients

About 20 medium-sized cookies

- 5 large organic eggs, at room temperature
- 4 ½ cups (450g) confectioners' sugar
- *1 teaspoon* pure anise oil or any natural flavor you like
- *6 cups (750g)* all-purpose flour (*3 ¾ cups (480g)* for the dough and the rest for dusting the work surface)

Method

Line two standard-sized baking sheets with parchment paper.

In the bowl of a stand mixer fitted with the whisk attachment, whip the eggs until very pale. Add the confectioners' sugar in 3 additions and whip until combined.

Switch to the paddle attachment and with the mixer on low, gradually add the flour and beat until combined. Gather the dough into a ball and on a well-floured surface, use a rolling pin to roll it out to 1 cm (⅜ inch) for standard molds or 1.27 cm (½ inch) for deeper molds.

Brush your springerle molds with flour every time you press them into your dough. Once you press the desired design into the dough, use a cookie cutter to cut it into shapes. Arrange the springerle on the parchment-lined baking sheet. (If you plan to hang the springerle to decorate your Christmas tree, now is the time to cut holes with a round piping tip so you can hang the cookies with ribbon on the tree. Keep in mind that the cookies will expand during baking, so choose a tip that fits the size of your springerle.) Cover the springerle with a kitchen cloth and let dry out at room temperature for at least 5 hours and preferably overnight.

Preheat the oven to 350°F (180°C).

Bake the springerle for 6 to 8 minutes for small to medium cookies, and up to 12 minutes for larger cookies or until pale in color, but golden on the bottom. Springerle can be stored in airtight containers for at least a week.

Eggnog

Thank you, Mr. Carl Joannessons, wherever you are right now, for inventing this drink, way back in 1700, while experimeting at the bar. I know for a fact that sometimes good things come from mistakes. How reassuring is that?

Ingredients

Makes about 6 servings

- *3* large organic eggs
- *3 tablespoons (40 g)* sugar
- *¼ teaspoon* salt
- *2 cups (480 ml)* whole milk
- *1 teaspoon* pure vanilla extract
- *¾ cup (180 ml)* whiskey, such as Balvenie Caribbean Cask 14-year-old single malt whiskey, or rum of your choice
- Ground nutmeg

Method

In a medium-sized saucepan, whisk the eggs, then add the sugar and salt and whisk to combine. Add 1 cup (240 ml) of the milk and cook on low heat, stirring constantly, for about 8 minutes, or until slightly thick. Stir in the remaining 1 cup (240 ml) of milk, along with the vanilla and whiskey. Remove from the heat, cover with plastic wrap, and refrigerate overnight. You can enjoy the eggnog in many different ways, it's up to your taste. It can be served piping hot in mugs, slightly warm in a nice glass, or cold straight from the fridge. However you choose, a sprinkle of nutmeg over the top provides extra flavor!

Sbrisolona di Mantova

Ingredients

6 servings

- *8 ounces (200g)* whole blanched almonds
- *1 ⅓ cups* plus *2 teaspoons (280g)* sugar
- *2 cups (260g)* all-purpose flour
- *1 ½ cups (250g)* polenta flour
- *1 cup* plus *2 tablespoons (250g)* unsalted butter, cold and cut into cubes
- Pinch of salt
- *3 medium* organic egg yolks
- Freshly-grated zest of *1* organic lemon
- *1 teaspoon* vanilla bean paste or pure vanilla extract
- *1 ½ ounces (40g)* whole almonds

Is this really a cake? Well, not really. Sbrisolona is a crumble made with hazelnuts that landed in Italy, at the Court of the Gonzaga family, around the year 600. It used to be called "3 cups cake" because the flours and sugar are measured in equal parts. This cake is never sliced. It must be eaten with your hands and possibly drenched in grappa for a full sensorial experience. This is one of those preparations in Italy that comes at the very end of a festive meal, after the other cakes are served. If it breaks while you're putting it on a serving plate, don't panic—it's meant to be fragile. If you are not into grappa, pair this cake with a good glass of Moscato wine, Persichetto Lunae, Vin Santo, Passito wine, or brandy liquor.

Method

Preheat the oven to 350°F (180°C) and butter and flour a 10-inch (25-cm) round pan.

In a blender, combine the blanched almonds and 1 ¼ cups (250g) of the sugar and pulse until chopped, but not fine. Transfer to a large bowl, add the all-purpose flour, polenta flour, butter, and salt, and mix everything together.

In a small bowl, stir together the egg yolks, lemon zest, and vanilla. Add to the almond and flour mixture and stir gently to combine. Pour the batter into the prepared pan without pressing or spreading it too much—you want an even but still crumbly texture. Sprinkle with the remaining 2 tablespoons plus 1 teaspoon (30g) sugar and the unpeeled almonds. Bake at 350°F (180°C) for 45 to 50 minutes or until golden. Let cool before serving.

Gianduiotto

Ingredients

*Makes 1 large gianduiotto
or 32 small ones*

- *16 ounces (400g)* good quality milk chocolate
- *8 ounces (200g)* good quality pure hazelnut spread
- A dollop of whipped cream (optional)

This recipe takes us to Piemonte, an Italian region famous around the world for its hazelnuts and chocolate. Gianduiotto is made with only these two ingredients, but you will never forget them. I know I will never forget my first gianduiotto, which I had when I was just five years old. It is traditional to make gianduiotti in individual molds, easily found online. However, in keeping with the theme of this book, which is all about gathering and sharing with the ones you love, I decided to use one large mold to create a big gianduiotto. The result is generous and demands to be shared. Smaller gianduiotto are for those little moments by yourself, after a long day at work, or when you're craving something sweet. They are meant to be enjoyed in the most positively selfish way! We need that too sometimes...

Method

Roughly chop 7 ounces (200g) of the chocolate. In a bain-marie or a metal bowl set over a pan of simmering water, melt the roughly chopped chocolate. Finely chop the remaining 7 ounces (200g) of chocolate, then add it to the melted chocolate and stir carefully to remove any air bubbles or unmelted bits. Add the hazelnut spread and stir thoroughly, then pour the mixture into a large silicone gianduiotto mold or small individual molds. Clean any excess around the edges of the mold, cover with plastic wrap, and let set at room temperature overnight. If your kicthen is too warm, you can refrigerate the gianduiotto, but be sure to remove it 30 minutes before serving and let sit at room temperature. Serve with a dollop of whipped cream on the side, if you like, and enjoy with a glass of coffee liqueur, if you please.

Torrone Al Cioccolato

CHOCOLATE NOUGAT

As with panettone and the pandoro, there are very distinct schools of thought on whether the best torrone is the white one made with honey and nuts, or the more modern version made with chocolate, hazelnuts, and sometimes even candied fruit. I think it's a matter of personal taste and, when in doubt, I usually satisfy all of my cravings by having a piece of each. You can make torrone in individual silicone molds and then wrap them in cute candy wrappers. They make wonderful little gifts!

Ingredients

*Enough for a party
of at least 5 people*

- *8 ounces (200g)* whole blanched hazelnuts
- *16 ounces (400g)* good quality dark chocolate, 70% cacao
- *14 ounces (350g)* milk chocolate
- *12 ounces (300g)* white chocolate
- *2 teaspoons* hazelnut liqueur, such as Frangelico (optional, but strongly suggested)
- *14 ounces (350g)* good quality hazelnut chocolate spread

Method

Spray a 10 ½-inch (26.5-cm) loaf tin with baking spray and line with parchment paper, making sure the paper adheres completely to the bottom and sides and that there no air pockets or creases.

In a large skillet over medium heat, toast the hazelnuts, occasionally shaking the pan, for about 15 minutes or until golden. Let cool at room temperature.

In a bain-marie or a metal bowl set over a pan of simmering water, melt the dark chocolate. Using a pastry brush, brush the melted dark chocolate onto the parchment paper inside the loaf tin. Refrigerate for 10 to 15 minutes or until the dark chocolate is dry. Repeat this step 3 times to create a thick layer of dark chocolate. Reserve some dark chocolate to coat the base later.

In a bain-marie or a metal bowl set over a pan of simmering water, melt the milk and white chocolate together. Add the hazelnut liqueur (if using), followed by the hazelnut spread and stir until creamy and well blended. Add the toasted hazelnuts and pour into the loaf tin. Cover with the reserved melted dark chocolate, using a spatula to smooth the surface. Cover and refrigerate for at least 4 hours.

Remove the torrone from the refrigerator and let it come to room temperature before serving.

Bonet

*I*n *my first book, "The Italian Baker," I talked about a restaurant in Sarzana, "Ottone I," owned by Remo and Lucia. I can't avoid mentioning Lucia again because she introduced me to this recipe, a dessert from the Piedmont region and a classic to this day! Her Bonet is incredible! As with all the desserts Lucia makes, I am a huge fan—can you tell? This is my version, and it is a tribute to Lucia and the kind of desserts she makes—wholesome, simple, real, and honest, which is exactly how I like my desserts to be! Bonet at Christmas is like a good Caprese salad in summer: a must!*

Ingredients

6 servings

- *1 ½ cups (300g)* sugar
- *1 ¼ cups (300ml)* whole milk
- *¾ cup* plus *2 tablespoons (210ml)* liquid whipping cream
- *1 ½ tablespoons* unsweetened cocoa powder
- *2 ½ ounces (65g)* good quality dark chocolate, chopped
- *3 large organic eggs*
- *6 ounces (150g)* Amaretti cookies, roughly crushed
- *1 teaspoon* rum

Method

Preheat the oven to 350°F (180°C).

Bring a medium-sized saucepan of water to a boil.

In a medium-sized saucepan over low heat, combine 1 ¼ cups (250g) of the sugar and ½ cup (120ml) of water and heat, without stirring or touching, until the sugar is completely melted and golden in color. Quickly pour the caramel inside a 4-cup (1-liter) loaf pan or any similarly sized mold, tilting the pan so the caramel evenly covers the entire surface. Let set at room temperature.

In a medium-sized pan over medium heat, bring the milk and whipping cream to a simmer. Mix in the cocoa powder and stir until combined, then mix in the chopped chocolate and stir until combined. Meanwhile, in the bowl of a stand mixer fitted with the whisk attachment or using a hand-held mixer, combine the eggs and the remaining ¼ cups (40g) of sugar and whip on medium speed until pale and fluffy. In a steady stream, pour the hot milk and cream mixture into the bowl and continue whipping until fully incorporated. Add the rum and crushed cookies and whip until stiff.

Pour the batter into the loaf pan, then place the loaf pan inside a slightly larger and deeper baking dish. Carefully pour enough of the boiling water inside the larger pan to come about halfway up the sides of the loaf pan, making sure the Bonet remains in the center of the larger baking dish. Carefully transfer both pans to the oven and bake for about 1 hour, or until completely set. Remove the loaf pan from the larger pan and refrigerate for at least 7 hours, or until completely set. To release the Bonet from its mold, run a blow torch quickly around the base of the mold and then invert the Bonet on a serving plate. If you don't have a blow torch, gently place the tin in a pan filled with boiling water for about 2 minutes and then invert it carefully on the serving plate. Enjoy!

Marquise au Chocolat

This is elegance in flavor and sin at its core. I imagine serving this dessert at a stylish Christmas dinner party, perhaps a friends' get-together right before leaving the city and heading back to your childhood home, where more traditional festivities are planned. I see it as a simple yet fancy, decadent and modern dessert (though it originated in France in 1671). According to legend, Marie de Rabutin Chantal, Marquis de Sévigné, was so in love with chocolate that she was literally obsessed with it. Of course, this is only legend, but whatever the occasion, or whatever the story, do yourself a favor and make this dessert. You will not be disappointed.

Note: This recipe uses raw eggs. Please use super fresh organic eggs or already pasteurized organic eggs (if availabale).

Gluten Free!

Ingredients

8/10 servings

- *14 ounces (350g)* good quality dark chocolate (minimum 65% cacao), finely chopped
- *¾ cup plus 1 ½ teaspoons (200ml)* double cream
- *¾ cup (170g)* unsalted butter, at room temperature
- *½ cup (100g)* granulated sugar
- *4 super fresh large organic eggs,* separated
- *1 teaspoon* vanilla bean paste or pure vanilla extract
- *1 ½ teaspoons* dark rum
- *1 teaspoon* unsweetened cocoa powder

Method

Line a 12 x 4.4 x 2.8-inch (30 x 11 x 7-cm) loaf pan with plastic wrap.

In a bain-marie or a metal bowl set over a pan of simmering water, melt the dark chocolate. Stir in the cream and let cool at room temperature.

In the bowl of a stand mixer fitted with the paddle attachment, combine the butter and sugar and beat on medium-high until light and fluffy. Add the egg yolks and stir to incorporate, then add the melted chocolate mixture, rum, and vanilla and beat until combined. Transfer to a large bowl.

Clean the bowl of the stand mixer and use the whisk attachment to whip the egg whites until very stiff, then gently fold them into the chocolate mixture. Pour into the prepared loaf pan and smooth the top. Freeze for at least 2 hours and preferably overnight.

Invert Marquise onto a serving plate, dust with cocoa powder, and decorate with gold leaf, or fruit if you prefer.

Mandorlaccio Di Altamura

ALMOND CAKE FROM ALTAMURA

Ingredients

About 8/10 slices

- *20 ounces (500g)* blanched almonds
- *1 cup* plus *2 tablespoons (225g)* sugar
- *2 ounces (50g)* acacia honey, or other clear liquid honey
- Freshly-grated zest of *1* organic lemon
- Freshly-grated zest of *1* organic orange
- *6* large organic eggs, separated
- *1 ½ teaspoons* baking powder
- Pinch of salt

For the glaze
- *8 ounces (200g)* white chocolate
- *8 ounces (200g)* almond praline

*P*uglia is celebrated for its gorgeous beaches, good wine, great food, and nice weather, but I think it isn't celebrated enough in the baking world. Big mistake! The region has many traditional recipes for sweets and this one is one of them. The North has Pandoro and Panettone, while the South has Mandorlaccio, along with many other interesting recipes. It is believed that the Mandorlaccio dates back to the pre-Roman era. Legend has it that this cake was baked to celebrate Mother Earth and the annual rebirth of the land. To this day in Puglia, the Mandorlaccio is always on the Christmas table! This is my version.

Method

Preheat the oven to 200°F (100°C). Line a baking sheet with parchment paper and spray the inside of an 8-inch (20-cm) half-sphere cake mold with baking spray.

Spread the almonds in an even layer on the parchment-lined baking sheet and bake for about 10 minutes or until toasted. Transfer to a blender, add 2 tablespoons of the sugar and blend until they resemble a fine flour.

Raise the oven temperature to 350°F (180°C).

In a small saucepan over medium heat, combine the honey with the lemon and orange zest and cook until slightly warm.

In the bowl of a stand mixer fitted with the paddle attachment, combine the egg yolks and the remaining 1 cup (200g) of sugar and beat on high speed until pale and doubled in volume. Add the warm honey mixture, the ground almond mixture, and the baking powder, and stir with a spatula to combine.

Clean the bowl of the stand mixer and use the whisk attachment to whip the egg whites until frothy. Add the salt and whip until stiff peaks form. Gently fold the egg whites into the batter, being careful not to deflate it, then pour into the prepared pan and bake for 50 to 55 minutes. After about 40 minutes, test the cake by inserting a toothpick in the center to see if it comes out clean. Let cool in the pan for about 20 minutes, then invert onto a wire rack.

Make the glaze in a bain-marie or a metal bowl set over a pan of simmering water. Melt the white chocolate and pour it over the entire surface of the cake and press the almond praline all over it. Arrange the cake on a serving plate and refrigerate for at least 1 hour in order to set the glaze before serving.

Budino Di Ricotta Alla Romana

RICOTTA PUDDING, THE ROMAN WAY

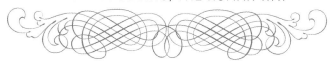

*A*t Christmas, Rome shines even more than usual. When I was a child, Sunday afternoons during the holiday season were my absolute favorite days. My family would start by strolling through the city center in search of presents. Of course, there was always time to enjoy chestnuts, which were roasted on an open fire and sold wrapped in paper at the corner of Piazza Di Spagna. They were so hot, I would literally burn my fingers peeling them, but I didn't mind—nothing could spoil a day like that!

Santa Claus was also there, riding his sleigh up and down Via del Corso, urging us kids to follow him to Piazza Navona, where the annual Christmas market still takes place today. There you find candies in every flavor and color, hot chocolate, and more roasted chestnuts, plus a carousel, toys, and Christmas carols to listen to and to sing. And it smells of cinnamon mixed with cotton candy.

For me, the most important moment was grabbing a slice of this traditional Roman dessert—the king of all ricotta desserts! I would stand in front of the food truck, eager to get my slice, thinking about how good it was to be a child at Christmas, while watching icing sugar be sprinkled—like snow over the mountains—on this yummy yet simple cake. I would beg my father, saying, "Papà! Me ne compri una? Per piacere!!" ("Daddy! Would you buy me one? Please!!!")

Memories like these stay with you forever—hence my love for anything made with ricotta and the reason why I use it so often in my recipes. Ricotta is a part of Rome the way a child is a part of its mother, which is why this traditional recipe earns a place in this book and deserves to be a new fa-vorite on your table, too. Moscato wine works magic with this type of dessert—you have my word.

Note: For this recipe, I usually use one part cow's milk ricotta and one part sheep's milk ricotta, but I understand finding sheep's milk ricotta can be difficult in some areas. Feel free to use all cow's milk ricotta, but please use the best you can find, as you will taste the difference.

Ingredients

6/8 servings

- A little softened butter, for greasing
- *20 ounces (500g)* super fresh ricotta
- *1 large organic egg* plus *4 large organic eggs,* separated
- *1 cup (200g)* granulated sugar
- *¼ cup* plus *1 tablespoon (40g)* all-purpose flour, sifted
- *2 teaspoons* vanilla bean paste or pure vanilla extract
- *1 teaspoon* ground cinnamon
- *1 ½ ounces (40g)* candied citrus peel
- Freshly-grated zest of *1* organic lemon
- *2 tablespoons* rum
- Confectioners' sugar to decorate

Method

Preheat the oven to 350°F (180°C). Butter and flour a 4-cup (1-liter) pudding tin or any similarly sized baking dish—even a loaf pan will work.

In a large bowl, strain the ricotta to remove any excess water, then transfer to a large bowl. Add the whole egg plus the 4 egg yolks and stir until fully combined. Add the granulated sugar, flour, vanilla, and cinnamon and mix thoroughly. Add the candied citrus and fold to incorporate the lemon zest.

In the bowl of a stand mixer fitted with the whisk attachment, whip the egg whites until stiff, then gently fold them into the ricotta mixture, being careful not to deflate it. Pour the batter into the prepared pudding tin and bake for 40–45 minutes or until golden. Let cool in the tin for at least 30 minutes, then flip the pudding onto a serving dish or wire rack. While the pudding is still warm, sprinkle with icing sugar and serve. If leftovers are well wrapped, they can be refrigerated for up to 2 days.

Torta Albero Di Natale

CHRISTMAS TREE CAKE

Ingredients

About 6/8 portions

- 2 ½ cups *(350g)* all-purpose flour
- 2 ¼ cups *(250g)* almond flour
- 2 *tablespoons* baking powder
- ½ *teaspoon* salt
- 1 ⅓ cups *(300g)* unsalted butter, at room temperature
- 1 ½ cups *(300g)* sugar
- 2 *tablespoons* rum
- 2 *teaspoons* vanilla bean paste or pure vanilla extract
- Freshly-grated zest of *2* organic oranges
- *5* large organic eggs, at room temperature
- ½ *cup (115ml)* milk, at room temperature
- *8 ounces (200g)* dried cranberries
- *8 ounces (200g)* candied orange peel, roughly chopped
- Sliced almonds
- Confectioners' sugar for dusting

*F*or this type of cake, it is very important that you don't overmix the batter or you will end up with a very tough cake, so only mix it enough to barely incorporate each ingredient. Don't worry if you see streaks of flour in the end—it will work just fine. This is an easy cake to make and yet it is very pretty to look at, thanks to the Christmas tree–shaped paper case. Fun to make and delicious to eat—what more do you need?

Method

Preheat the oven to 350°F (180°C). Place a 36-ounce (900-g) Christmas tree–shaped paper mold on a baking sheet.

In a large bowl, sift together the all-purpose flour, almond flour, baking powder, and salt.

In the bowl of a stand mixer fitted with the paddle attachment or using a hand-held mixer, beat the butter and sugar until pale and fluffy. Add the rum, vanilla, and orange zest and beat until incorporated. Add the eggs, 1 at a time, and beat until incorporated. Add the flour mixture in 3 additions, beating until barely incorporated. Add the milk and stir by hand using a spatula. Gently fold the mixture by hand, then fold in the cranberries and candied orange. Pour the batter into the prepared mold and spread the batter using a spatula. Sprinkle with sliced almonds and bake for about 45 minutes, or until a wooden toothpick inserted in the center of the cake comes out clean. Let the cake cool in the mold. Dust with a little confectioners' sugar and serve with a dollop of vanilla ice cream and a glass of brandy. I eat it just like this and it tastes marvelous!

Brandy Custard

Ingredients

6 Servings

- *2 ⅓ cups (555ml)* whole milk
- *¾ cup (180ml)* light cream (18 % fat)
- *4 large organic egg yolks*
- *½ cup (100g)* sugar
- *1 ½ tablespoons* organic cornstarch
- *¼ cup (60ml)* brandy

*A*lthough this is not a full desert on its own, it needs to be added to your Christmas recipe book. Brandy is one of those delicious liqueurs that's not widely popular when ordering a drink, but during the holiday season, gets some well-deserved respect! I think it's an important ingredient, along with rum, to have on hand for baking. This is a versatile brandy custard you can pour over many of the recipes in this book. You can also serve it warm over vanilla ice cream, or perhaps dip ginger cookies in it. However you enjoy this custard, do yourself a favor and simply make it. I am sure there will always be a good use for it.

Method

In a medium-sized saucepan over medium heat, warm the milk and cream for about 5 minutes or until gently simmering. Remove from the heat and set aside.

In a medium-sized bowl, whisk together the egg yolks, sugar, and cornstarch until fully incorporated and pale in color. Add the egg yolk mixture to the milk and cream. Place over medium heat and stir constantly for about 4 minutes, or until thickened but not fully boiling. Remove from the heat, add the brandy and stir to incorporate. Cover with plastic wrap and let cool at room temperature until warm to the touch, then refrigerate until cold. When ready to use, warm the custard in a medium-sized saucepan over medium heat or serve it cold.

Il Mio Strudel Alla Ricotta E Cioccolato

MY CHOCOLATE AND RICOTTA STRUDEL

Ingredients

6 servings

For the dough
- *1 ¾ cups* plus *3 tablespoons (250g)* all-purpose flour
- *1* large organic egg
- *⅓ cup* plus *1 tablespoon (90ml)* water, lukewarm
- *1 tablespoon* vegetable oil
- Pinch of salt
- *1 teaspoon (5ml)* white vinegar

For the filling
- *¼ cup* plus *2 teaspoons (70g)* unsalted butter
- *Two handfuls (50g)* breadcrumbs
- *18 ounces (450g)* ricotta cheese
- *¼ cup* plus *3 tablespoons (90g)* sugar
- *2 tablespoons* dark cocoa powder
- *4 ¾ ounces (120g)* small dark chocolate chips
- *1 tablespoon* rum
- *1 teaspoon* vanilla bean paste or pure vanilla extract
- *4 ¾ ounces (120g)* Amaretti cookies, roughly crushed
- *3 tablespoons* unsalted butter, melted (to seal the dough)
- *1* organic egg, beaten (for the egg wash)
- more cocoa powder, for dusting

*W*ait a minute! Chocolate strudel??? Yes, but allow me to explain. When I lived in Germany, and the many other times I visited, I enjoyed the best strudel ever! And because Germans know all about good cakes, I decided to create a variation that celebrates a German classic without stomping on their traditions! So, please excuse me for being brave enough to enter the mystical world of strudel and its many variations in flavor. I love it and I think it should be baked more and more! I leave the real deal to German grandmothers; I hope to meet one of them one day, so I can ask for their strudel secrets And me, well, I like chocolate so... go figure!

Method

Make the dough by placing the flour in a large bowl and making a well in the center. Put the egg, lukewarm water, oil, and salt in the well, then add the vinegar and knead until a smooth dough forms—work quickly so the vinegar doesn't have time to curdle the egg. Wrap the dough in a clean dishtowel and let rest at room temperature for about 30 minutes.

Preheat the oven to 350°F (180°C) and line a baking sheet with parchment paper.

Make the filling in a medium-sized saucepan over medium heat. First melt the butter. Add the breadcrumbs and toast, stirringing, until golden in color. Let cool.

In a large bowl, combine the ricotta, sugar, cocoa powder, and chocolate chips. Use a rubber spatula to fold until fully incorporated, then add the rum and vanilla and stir to combine. Add the cooled breadcrumbs and the crushed Amaretti cookies and stir to incorporate.

On a lightly-floured dishtowel, use a rolling pin to roll out the dough into a very thin rectangle. Without rolling the dough off of the kitchen cloth, try to roll it as thin as possible, so it is almost see-through. (The thinner you roll the dough, the better your strudel will be.) This type of dough is very elastic and if it is kneaded properly, it will not break.

Spread the filling in the center of the rectangle of dough, then use the kitchen cloth to lift up the ends and roll up everything to form a log shape. Brush the borders of the dough with melted butter and press the edges together to seal the strudel. Carefully lift up the strudel and arrange it on the baking sheet. Using a pastry brush, brush the entire surface with the lightly-beaten egg. This will create a golden crust during baking. Using a sharp knife, make three incisions so the steam will be released during baking. Bake for 40 to 45 minutes or until golden. Let cool to room temperature, then dust with cocoa powder and decorate with berries to make it even more festive!

Torta Bonissima

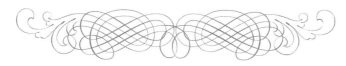

Ingredients

8 servings

For the sugar crust
- *3 sticks (340g)* unsalted butter, at room temperature plus more to butter the tart pan
- *1 ⅓ cups* plus *1 tablespoon (280g)* sugar
- Freshly-grated zest of *1* organic lemon
- Pinch of salt
- *1 teaspoon* vanilla bean paste or pure vanilla extract
- *2 large* organic eggs
- *4 large* organic egg yolks
- *5 cups (600g)* all-purpose flour plus *2 tablespoons* to flour the tart pan
- *½ teaspoon* baking powder

For the filling
- *16 ounces (400g)* walnuts
- *16 ounces (400g)* clear liquid honey, such as Acacia
- *2 tablespoons* rum

For the glaze
- *10 ounces (250g)* good quality dark chocolate (minimum 65% cacao)
- *2 tablespoons* white wine
- Walnuts, crushed

*T*he name of this cake is from a dialect of the Emilia-Romagna region, and more specifically, from the city of Modena, where this cake is baked every year during the holiday season. Bonissima translates as "super good." The story behind this cake is that a very wealthy noblewoman enlisted the help of other nobles to feed all the starving people during a long famine. When the famine finally ended, she decided to celebrate by throwing a big party and invited only the people who had actually helped. She dedicated this cake, as well as a statue in Modena, to all of the amazing people who help others every day of the year. Now I share this recipe as another dedication to all of those generous spirits who represent the essence of Christmas.

Method

Make the pastry in the bowl of a stand mixer fitted with the paddle attachment. Combine the butter, sugar, lemon zest, and salt and beat until combined. Add the whole eggs and the egg yolks and beat until fully incorporated. Add the flour and baking powder and beat until a dough forms. On a work surface, knead the dough to form a ball. Cover in plastic wrap and refrigerate for at least 3 hours and preferably overnight.

Make the filling in a food processor or blender. Pulse the walnuts until roughly crushed, then transfer to a large bowl, add the honey and rum and stir until fully combined.

Preheat the oven to 350°F (180°C). Butter and flour a 9 ½-inch (24-cm) fluted tart pan with a removable bottom.

Divide the pastry into 2 even portions. On a lightly-floured work surface, use a rolling pin to roll out each piece of dough into a 1/4-inch (3-mm) thick round. Carefully wrap one round of dough around the rolling pin and unroll it over the prepared tart pan. Press the dough into the bottom and sides of the pan and trim any excess dough. Fill the tart with the walnut filling, then cover with the second round of dough, tucking the edges inwards to create a ridge that will work as a barrier and seal the tart. Using a fork, prick the entire surface to release steam during baking. Bake for about 40 minutes or until the pastry is golden. Let cool completely.

Make the glaze in a bain-marie or a metal bowl set over a pan of simmering water. Melt the chocolate, white wine, and 2 tablespoons of water, stirring constantly. Pour the glaze into the center of the tart, not allowing it to go over the sides. Let the glaze set at room temperature, then scatter it with walnuts for a final decorative touch.

Polvorones

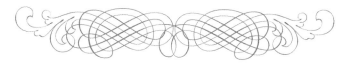

Ingredients

Makes about 20 cookies

- *3 ¾ cups (500g)* all-purpose flour
- *5 ounces (125g)* whole blanched almonds
- *1 ¼ cups (280g)* unsalted butter, at room temperature
- *2 ½ cups (250g)* confectioners' sugar, plus more for dusting
- *1 ½ teaspoons* ground cinnamon
- *1 teaspoon* vanilla bean paste or pure vanilla extract

*W*ith this Christmas recipe, I'm taking you to Spain. These cookies have a texture similar to French Sablé cookies, but they also remind me a little of Italian "Baci di Dama" (although they are very different from Polvorones, but still I taste slight similarities). The original recipe calls for lard, but being vegetarian, I don't bake with animal products like gelatin or lard, so I use butter. You can choose lard if you prefer—there's no judgment. Whatever you decide, I strongly suggest you make these delicious cookies. I make them for Christmas, but also for any time of year— they are perfect for afternoon tea, too!

Method

Set a rack in the lower third of the oven and preheat the oven to 325°F (160°C). Line a baking sheet with parchment paper.

Spread the almonds on the sheet. Toast them on the lower rack of the oven (be careful not to burn the almonds) for about 15 minutes or until golden. Let cool at room temperature, then transfer the cooled almonds to a blender and pulse until just crushed, but not too fine.

In the bowl of a stand mixer fitted with the paddle attachment, beat the butter until creamy. Add the confectioners' sugar, cinnamon, vanilla, and the flour and almond mixture, and beat until a dough forms. The dough will be very crumbly. This type of dough is meant to be that way. Place the dough between 2 sheets of parchment paper and use a rolling pin to roll out the dough until about ¾-inch (2-cm) thick. Rest the dough in the refrigerator for at least 3 hours.

Using 1 ¼ to 1 ½-inch (3 to 4-cm) round cutters, cut the dough into circles and then transfer to baking sheets. Bake for about 20 minutes, depending on the size of the cookies, or until lightly golden on the edges but still pale in the center. Let cool completely on the sheet before touching the cookies, then dust with confectioners' sugar.

Pumpkin Spice Cake

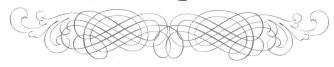

Ingredients

About 6/8 slices

- *16 ounces (400g)* fresh pumpkin, cut into chunks
- *3 cups (390g)* all-purpose flour, sifted
- *2 teaspoons* baking powder
- *¼ teaspoon* salt
- *4* large organic eggs, at room temperature
- *1 ¼ cups (250g)* granulated sugar
- *⅓ cup* plus *1 tablespoon* plus *1 teaspoon (100ml)* vegetable oil
- *2 tablespoons* rum
- *1 ½ teaspoons* ground cinnamon
- *1 teaspoon* vanilla bean paste or pure vanilla extract
- *4 ¾ ounces (120g)* good quality dark chocolate chips
- Confectioners' sugar, to decorate

I know pumpkins are an autumn symbol, but I think they should stick with us throughout winter, too! They are beautiful to look at, versatile to cook with, and they make great home decorations. If I ever write a book about savory food, I promise to share my amazing recipe for pumpkin and Champagne risotto, as it never fails to impress. But for now, let's stick to Christmas sweet treats like my Italian version of pumpkin spice cake. It's perfect for breakfast, or in place of panettone, pandoro, or any traditional cake served at the end of the meal. Get creative and dress the cake with fresh cranberries, dried cranberries, or even fir or pine cones. You can also wrap a nice red ribbon around it for a Victorian look!

Method

Preheat the oven to 425°F (220°C) and line a baking sheet with parchment paper. Butter a 9-inch (23-cm) springform pan and line it with parchment paper.

Spread the pumpkin in an even layer on the parchment-lined baking sheet and bake for 25 to 30 minutes, or until soft and tender. Transfer to a blender and blend until creamy. Lower the oven temperature to 350°F (180°C).

In a large bowl, whisk together the flour, baking powder, and salt.

In the bowl of a stand mixer fitted with the whisk attachment or using a hand-held mixer, whip the eggs and sugar until tripled in volume. With the mixer on low speed, in a slow, steady stream, add the oil and then add the rum, cinnamon, and vanilla and whip until incorporated. Add the pumpkin puree. Finally, add the flour mixture and fold by hand until just incorporated. Fold in the chocolate chips. Pour the batter into the prepared pan and bake for about 45 minutes, or until a wooden toothpick inserted in the center of the cake comes out clean. Let cool at room temperature, then invert onto a serving plate or cake stand. Dust with confectioners' sugar and decorate as you please.

Champagne Jelly

Ingredients

4 Champagne glasses

- *1 (25.4-ounce / 750ml)* bottle rosé Champagne
- *3 ¼ ounces (90g)* clear liquid honey
- *2 teaspoons* agar agar powder
- Raspberries, to decorate
- Gold leaf, to decorate (optional)

*C*hampagne defines holiday parties like no other drink. Wherever there are bubbles involved, you can be sure there is a celebration happening! And so, another excuse to have Champagne is to turn it into a solid form and make it even more stylish— as if Champagne wasn't stylish enough! I use rosé Champagne for this recipe, but feel free to use regular Champagne, too. This recipe uses agar agar, so as always, it is vegetarian.

Method

In a medium-sized saucepan, stir together the Champagne and honey. Add the agar agar powder and bring to a boil. Let cook for 1 minute and then strain through a sieve. Drop 1 or 2 raspberries at the bottom of a Champagne flute, a Champagne coupe, or if you prefer, a martini glass. After pouring the jelly in, let it cool at room temperature until set, then serve immediately or refrigerate if you wish to serve it chilled. Decorate with additional raspberries or gold leaf for an even more glamorous finish!

Torta Chiffon Al Cacao

COCOA CHIFFON CAKE

Ingredients

12 servings

- *3 cups plus 2 ½ tablespoons (500g)* rice flour
- *2 cups (240g)* wheat starch or organic cornstarch
- *1 ¼ cups (125g)* unsweetened dark cocoa powder
- *2 teaspoons* baking powder
- *¼ teaspoon* salt
- *1 ¾ cups (360g)* sugar, divided
- *8 large organic egg yolks plus 10 large organic egg whites,* at room temperature
- *1 cup plus 1 tablespoon (250ml)* organic sunflower oil
- *2 cups plus 1 tablespoon (500ml)* lukewarm water
- *2 teaspoons* vanilla bean paste or pure vanilla extract
- *½ teaspoon* cream of tartar

*E*veryone should enjoy a good slice of cake whenever they please, but at Christmas it is a must! Often people who are gluten intolerant are destined to many restrictions, but not this time. This a base recipe to keep on hand and a wonderful start to create endless combinations! So, now it's your time to be creative in the kitchen. I'm sure it will be amazing!

Method

Preheat the oven to 350°F (180°C). Spray a chiffon cake pan or 2 8-inch (20-cm) round cake pans with baking spray.

In a large bowl, whisk together the rice flour, organic cornstarch, ¾ cup plus 2 tablespoons (180g) of the sugar, the cocoa powder, baking powder, and salt. Add the egg yolks, sunflower oil, vanilla, and the warm water and mix to combine. The mixture will be very thick. (This happens when using rice flour, so don't worry.)

In the bowl of a stand mixer fitted with the whisk attachment, combine the egg whites and cream of tartar and whip until frothy. Add the remaining ¾ cup plus 2 tablespoons (180g) of sugar and beat until stiff peaks form. Add a small amount of the meringue into the rice flour mixture. Beat using your mixer on medium speed until fully combined. Stop the machine and add the remaining meringue, gently folding it in with a spatula until fully combined, being careful not to deflate the batter. Note that using two pans cuts down on the baking time. Pour the batter into the prepared pan and bake for about 40 minutes, or until a toothpick inserted in the center comes out clean. Leave in the pan until the cake is cool enough to touch, then invert onto a wire rack to cool completely. Decorate as you desire and serve.

Sherry Cake

Ingredients

For the cake
- *1 ½ cups (195g)* all-purpose flour, sifted
- *2 teaspoons* baking powder
- Pinch of salt
- *⅓ cup plus 2 tablespoons (100ml)* whole milk
- Freshly-squeezed juice of *1* organic lemon
- *⅓ cup plus 1 tablespoon (90g)* unsalted butter, at room temperature
- *1 cup plus 2 tablespoons (220g)* sugar
- *1 teaspoon* vanilla bean paste or pure vanilla extract
- *1 teaspoon* ground cardamom
- *3* large organic eggs
- *⅔ cup (150ml)* sherry

For the glaze
- *¼ cup plus 3 tablespoons (80g)* sugar
- *¼ cup (60ml)* sherry
- *1 teaspoon* pure vanilla extract

I consider myself a modern girl with an old fashion taste. I love technology, but I'm also crazy about all things antique! I also like to rediscover and give new life to ingredients that seem to have been forgotten. Sherry is one of them, along with brandy. Thankfully, Christmas is a time when these two elegant drinks reach international stardom again! Ladies of the past used to drink sherry while getting warm in front of the fire after taking a walk in the country. And gentlemen traditionally drank brandy after dinner while smoking a cigar and talking about politics and life. How wonderful! This is my contribution to help sherry become a staple ingredient during your baking adventures! Bundt cakes shout Christmas to me, but choose any pan you like, as long as it holds eight cups of batter.

Method

Preheat the oven to 325°F (160°C). Butter and flour a pan that will hold 8 cups of batter.

In a large bowl, sift together the flour, baking powder, and salt.

In a small bowl, combine the milk and lemon juice.

In the bowl of a stand mixer fitted with the paddle attachment, combine the butter and sugar and beat until pale and fluffy. Add the eggs and beat until incorporated. Next add the vanilla and cardamom and beat to combine. Add the flour and milk mixtures in 3 additions, starting and ending with the flour, and beat until just combined. Add the sherry and stir by hand, using a spatula. Pour into the prepared pan and bake for about 1 hour, or until a wooden toothpick inserted in the center of the cake comes out clean. Let cool in the pan while you make the glaze.

Make the glaze in a small saucepan over medium heat. Combine the sugar, sherry, and vanilla and cook until the sugar is completely dissolved.

While the cake is still warm, invert onto a serving plate or cake board. Pour the glaze over the entire cake, then cut into slices and serve.

Torta Di Castagne E Cioccolato

CHESTNUT AND CHOCOLATE CAKE

Gluten Free!

Ingredients

6/8 servings

- *½ cup* plus *2 teaspoons (125g)* unsalted butter
- *4 ounces (100g)* good quality dark chocolate (minimum 60% cacao)
- *4* large organic eggs, separated
- *20 ounces (500g)* chestnut cream or chestnut jam
- *1 tablespoon* Amaretto
- *1 ½ teaspoons* pure vanilla extract
- *¼ teaspoon* cream of tartar
- Marron glacè and chocolate shavings, to decorate

*"*C*hestnuts roasting on an open fire, Jack Frost nipping at your nose..."* As I write this recipe, Nat King Cole is playing in the background. I love Christmas songs!!! They make the holidays even more magical! And Nat King Cole is the indisputable king of Christmas songs! Of course, I had to include a chestnut cake in this book, and this one is not only easy—even for beginners—but it's also gluten free! Yay! So, there is something for all and something for me too, because I love chestnuts! Happy Christmas to all!!!!*

Method

Preheat the oven to 350°F (180°C) and line the bottom and sides of a 9-inch (23-cm) round baking pan with parchment paper. Alternatively, spray the pan with gluten-free baking spray and line only the bottom with parchment paper.

In a bain-marie or a metal bowl set over a pan of simmering water, melt the butter and chocolate. Let cool at room temperature, then fold in the egg yolks, chestnut cream, amaretto, and vanilla.

Using a hand-held mixer, whip the egg whites and cream of tartar until stiff peaks form, then gently fold into the chocolate mixture. Pour into the prepared pan and bake for 30 to 35 minutes, or until a toothpick inserted in the center comes out clean. Remove from the oven and after 5 minutes, invert the cake onto a wire rack. Let completely cool at room temperature.

Decorate with fresh marron glacè and chocolate shavings, cut into slices, and serve.

Pan D'Arancio
ORANGE BREAD

Ingredients

About 8/10 Servings

For the vanilla-citrus juice
- Freshly-grated zest and freshly-squeezed juice of 2 organic oranges
- Freshly-grated zest and freshly-squeezed juice of 2 organic lemons
- *1 teaspoon* pure vanilla extract

For the cake
- *1 ½ cups* plus *2 tablespoons (325g)* sugar
- *1* organic orange, thinly sliced
- *2 ¼ cups (290g)* all-purpose flour, sifted
- *1 tablespoon* baking powder
- *½ teaspoon* salt
- *5* large organic eggs
- *1 teaspoon* pure vanilla extract
- Freshly-grated zest of *1* large organic orange
- *1 ½ teaspoons* orange-flavored liqueur, such as Grand Marnier
- *1 ⅓ cups (300g)* unsalted butter, melted and cooled

To decorate
- *6 tablespoons (150g)* orange marmalade, warmed and strained to remove chunks

I absolutely adore this cake! It's called "orange bread," but it's actually an up-side-down cake. The reason I call it pan d'arancio is because it combines two of my favorite recipes: an orange loaf bread that I make in my shop and an upside-down coffee cake. I am very happy with the resulting cake and I hope you will be, too! Christmas is full of orange scents and flavors, so if you want to swap out oranges for lemons, feel free to do so, but oranges work beautifully for this recipe!

Method

Make the vanilla-citrus juice in a small bowl by combining the orange and lemon zest and juice with the vanilla, and let stand at room temperature for 30 minutes.

Preheat the oven to 325°F (160°C). Butter a 10-inch (25-cm) springform pan and line the bottom with parchment paper.

Sprinkle ½ tablespoon of the sugar in the bottom of the parchment-lined pan and arrange the orange slices on the bottom of the pan, cutting the slices into small triangular pieces as needed to fill in the gaps. Sprinkle 1 ½ tablespoons of the sugar over the orange slices.

In a medium-sized bowl, sift together the flour, baking powder, and salt.

In the bowl of a stand mixer fitted with the whisk attachment, combine the eggs and the remaining 1 ½ cups (300 g) of sugar and whip until pale and tripled in volume. Add the vanilla, orange zest, and orange-flavored liqueur (if using), then beat to combine. With the mixer on low, add the melted and cooled butter in a slow, steady stream. Add the vanilla-citrus juice and whip to incorporate, then add the flour mixture and whip until just combined. Pour over the oranges in the pan and bake for about about 45 minutes, or until a wooden toothpick inserted in the center of the cake comes out clean. Let cool in the pan for 15 minutes, then invert onto a wire rack. While the cake is still warm, brush the entire surface with the orange marmalade, then cut into slices and serve.

Orange and Polenta Cake

Gluten Free!

Ingredients

About 8 slices

For the cake
- 2 organic oranges plus the freshly-grated zest of 1 organic orange
- 1 ½ cups (175g) almond flour
- ¾ cups (100g) polenta flour
- 1 tablespoon (5g) baking powder
- 5 large organic eggs
- 1 ¼ cups (250g) sugar
- 1 teaspoon vanilla bean paste or pure vanilla extract

For the orange syrup
- 1 cup (200g) sugar
- Freshly-squeezed juice of 4 organic oranges
- 1 teaspoon vanilla bean paste or pure vanilla extract
- 2 tablespoons plus 2 teaspoons (40ml) orange-flavored liqueur, such as Grand Marnier

When I bake this in my shop, it flies off the shelf! It is moist, packed with amazing orange flavor, and gluten free. Vitamin C? Oh, there's plenty in there. I add Grand Marnier to the syrup, but you can skip it if you don't like it. There is nothing more to say about this cake. It speaks for itself, trust me.

Method

Preheat the oven to 350°F (180°C) and line a 10-inch (25-cm) round cake pan with parchment paper.

Fill a medium-sized saucepan with water and set over medium heat. Peel 2 of the oranges, add them to the hot water, bring to a boil and cook for about 5 minutes (or until soft, but not overcooked because that is when they start to break). Transfer the oranges to a food processor or blender. Set aside to cool at room temperature.

In a large bowl, sift together the almond flour, polenta flour, and baking powder.

In the bowl of a stand mixer fitted with the whisk attachment, combine the eggs and sugar and whip until tripled in volume. Add the orange zest and vanilla, then very gently fold in the flour mixture. Finally, add the orange puree and stir until combined. Pour into the prepared pan and bake for 35 to 40 minutes, or until a toothpick inserted in the center of the cake comes out clean.

Make the orange syrup in a small saucepan. Bring the sugar, orange juice, vanilla, orange-flavored liqueur (if using), and ¼ cup (60ml) of water to a boil, then cook until syrupy. Let cool at room temperature.

While the cake is still warm and in the pan, pour the syrup all over the cake. Let the cake cool completely in the pan, then invert onto a wire rack or serving plate. Decorate with rose petals, candied orange zest, and if available, a dollop or quenelle of crème fraîche, tangy full-fat Greek yogurt, or any cream with a little acidity to contrast the sweetness of the cake.

Biscotti Di Natale Vegani
VEGAN CHRISTMAS COOKIES

Ingredients

Makes 5 medium-sized sandwich cookies

- *2 ⅜ cups (300g)* whole spelt flour or any other vegan flour
- *¼ cup* plus *3 tablespoons (90g)* pure unrefined cane sugar or any other vegan sugar
- Freshly-grated zest of *1* organic lemon
- *1 teaspoon* vanilla bean paste or pure vanilla extract
- *1 teaspoon* baking powder
- *½ teaspoon* ground cinnamon
- Pinch of salt
- *⅓ cup* plus *2 tablespoons (112ml)* organic vegetable oil
- *¼ cup (60ml)* cold almond milk, plus more as needed
- *10 ounces (250g)* good quality vegan raspberry jam, preferably homemade
- Vegan confectioners' sugar, for dusting

Vegan friends, this recipe is for you, and I guarantee it is a delicious one! You can save this recipe in your recipe notebook and use it as a base for other flavor combinations. Make the cookies one day ahead, so the jam has enough time to stick to the cookies. Alternatively, you can skip the jam and cut out single cookies, or you can fill them with vegan chocolate and hazelnut spread. Whatever your choice, bake this recipe all year round! You can double or triple the recipe as you please and make big batches for friends and family.

Method

In a large bowl, combine the spelt flour, pure unrefined cane sugar, lemon zest, vanilla, baking powder, cinnamon, and salt. Add the vegetable oil and almond milk and knead by hand until a dough forms. If the dough is too dry, gradually knead in a bit more almond milk. Wrap the dough in plastic wrap and let rest in the refrigerator for 1 hour.

Preheat the oven to 350°F (180°C) and line a baking sheet with parchment paper.

On a work surface, place the dough between 2 sheets of parchment paper and use a rolling pin to roll out until about ¼-inch (0.5-cm) thick. Divide the dough in half. Roll the dough to a 3 mm thickness. Use your chosen cutter and cut the desired shapes. You should have 10 cookies in total. Reserve five on the side. Using a smaller cutter of either the same shape or different (it can be a star, a heart or whatever you like), cut out the center of the other 5 cookies left. Transfer the cookies to the parchment-lined baking sheets and bake for 8–10 minutes or until until slightly golden. Let cool completely on the baking sheets.

Spread a little jam on the larger cookies, then top with the smaller cookies to create sandwiches. Dust with vegan confectioners' sugar.

Mostaccioli di Napoli

Ingredients

12/15 servings

- *1 ¾ ounces (45g)* chopped almonds
- *2 ⅓ cups (300g)* all-purpose flour
- *½ cup (100g)* sugar
- *¼ cup (25g)* unsweetened cocoa powder
- *1 teaspoon* baking soda
- *1 teaspoon (4g)* pisto or a mix of ground cinnamon, coriander, nutmeg, and cloves
- Freshly-grated zest of *1* large organic orange
- *3 tablespoons* freshly-squeezed orange juice
- *1 ¼ ounces (30g)* clear liquid honey
- *⅓ cup plus 2 tablespoons (100ml)* water, at room temperature
- *16 ounces (400g)* good quality dark chocolate (65% cacao minimum)

*T*hese soft, strange-looking treats are part cookie and part cake and they come from Naples. They are prepared using a particular mix of spices called "pisto," and dipped in a delicious chocolate glaze. The history around them goes back to the Middle Ages, when it was common to prepare them for the holidays, as it still is today. The word "mostaccioli" comes from the Latin "mosto," which refers to the maceration of grapes, one of the original ingredients. Today, it's very difficult to find this ingredient, so this modern version is made without it, but they are still delicious! Traditionally, mostaccioli di Napoli are made starting on December 8th, the day that officially opens the festive season. They last quite a while, and for this reason, they can be made ahead of time. If wrapped in colorful paper, they also make wonderful gifts.

Method

Preheat the oven to 300°F (150°C) and line 2 baking sheets with parchment paper.

Spread the almonds in an even layer on a parchment-lined baking sheet and toast for 5 to 10 minutes to release their precious oils. Let cool. Raise the oven temperature to 350°F (175°C).

In the bowl of a stand mixer fitted with the dough hook attachment, combine the flour, sugar, cocoa powder, baking soda, and pisto, along with the orange zest and juice, honey, and the water. Knead until a dough forms and doesn't stick to the sides of the bowl. Gather the dough into a ball, wrap in plastic wrap, and let rest at room temperature for 15 to 30 minutes.

Pat the dough flat between 2 sheets of parchment paper, then use a rolling pin to roll it out until about ½-inch (1.25-cm) thick. Using a rhombus cutter (or if you feel confident, just a knife), cut the dough into the desired shapes and transfer to the other parchment-lined baking sheet. Bake for 13 to 15 minutes. Let cool completely on the baking sheet.

In a bain-marie or a metal bowl set over a pan of simmering water, melt the dark chocolate. Alternatively, melt the chocolate in the microwave in 5-second intervals.

Using long pastry tweezers, lift each cookie and dip it into the melted chocolate, then place on a sheet of parchment paper and let set at room temperature. Once set, use a sharp knife to trim any excess chocolate.

Espresso Freddo

COLD ESPRESSO MOUSSE

Ingredients

Makes 8 servings

- *4* large super fresh organic eggs
- *¼ cup (30g)* all-purpose flour
- *2 teaspoons* vanilla bean paste or pure vanilla extract
- *1 teaspoon* baking powder
- *¼ teaspoon* salt
- *⅓ cup (80ml)* strong-brewed espresso coffee, cold
- *1 tablespoon* coffee liqueur, such as Kahlua
- *2 cups* plus *1 tablespoon (500ml)* heavy cream
- Cacao powder, to decorate (optional)

*W*ho doesn't like coffee? While some do not, for the majority of people, coffee is simply a divine drink. Italians enjoy coffee at any time of day, but particularly after a meal. And during the holidays, when friends and family gather at the table, moka machines never stop making that unmistakable sound—like a train arriving at the station! And it makes the house smell wonderful! This recipe is meant to be served cold and it can be accompanied by a shot of grappa or any liqueur you like. Pure bliss.

Method

In a medium-sized bowl, combine the eggs, flour, vanilla, salt, and baking pow-der and whisk until fully combined. Cover and refrigerate until ready to use.

In a small bowl, combine the espresso and coffee liqueur.

In the bowl of a stand mixer fitted with the whisk attachment or using a hand-held mixer, whip the heavy cream until stiff peaks form. Gently fold the the whipped cream into the chilled egg mixture.

Add the espresso mixture and stir until combined.

Fill 8 small bowls or glasses with the chocolate mousse and refrigerate for at least 2 hours and no longer than 8 hours. It is best to serve it on the same day. Dust with cocoa powder (if using), right before serving.

Christmas
BREADS
& Other Pastries

Brazadela

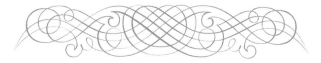

Ingredients

10/12 cantucci cookies

- *2 ⅓ cups (300g)* all-purpose flour
- *¾ cup (150g)* granulated sugar
- *⅓ cup* plus *1 tablespoon (90g)* butter, cut into small pieces and at room temperature
- *2* large organic eggs
- Freshly-grated zest of *1* organic lemon
- *1 teaspoon* anise-flavored liqueur (optional)
- *1 ½ teaspoons* baking powder
- *¼ teaspoon* salt
- *1 tablespoon* whole milk plus more as needed
- Pearl sugar, to decorate

*T*his cake comes from Ferrara, a city in Emilia-Romagna, and is a very old recipe from the region. In fact, brazadela dates back to 1250. It used to be, and still is, prepared for Christmas and other special occasions. Brazadela is a humble recipe. During those early years, chocolate was very expensive, so this cake was a good way to make something special without spending too much. The name brazadela comes from the dialect of the area and translates to "arm." Traditionally, brazadela was held under the left arm for serving, while the right hand poured wine. It is fascinating to me how these kinds of customs start, develop, and sometimes remain unchanged.

Method

Preheat the oven to (350 °F) 180°C and line a baking sheet with parchment paper.

Place the flour on a work surface and create a large well in the center - you should almost see the work surface and there should be a complete barrier around it so the ingredients won't spill from the sides. Add the granulated sugar, butter, eggs, lemon zest, liqueur (if using), baking powder, salt, and milk to the center of the well, then use your hands or a fork to begin blending the ingredients together. Slowly bring the flour from the sides of the well toward the center. Once the dough starts coming together, use your hands and knead it into a ball. If the dough is too dry, add a little more milk. Once a semi-soft dough forms, shape it into a ball, then flatten it a little using your hands and shape into a rectangle. Flour your hands and shape the dough into 2 medium-sized or 1 large roll. Arrange the roll or rolls on the parchment-lined baking sheet and flatten a little with your hands. Brush some milk over the entire surface, sprinkle with pearl sugar, and bake for about 30 minutes or until lightly golden in color, but not too dark. Let cool at room temperature, then cut diagonally like you would cut biscotti.

Popovers Per La Colazione Di Natale

CHRISTMAS MORNING BREAKFAST POPOVERS

Ingredients

12 popovers

- *2 cups (480ml)* whole milk
- *6* large organic eggs, at room temperature
- *2 tablespoons* unsalted butter, melted
- *2 cups* plus *2 tablespoons (280g)* all-purpose flour
- *1 teaspoon* baking powder
- *½ teaspoon* salt

To decorate
- *1 cup (200 g)* sugar
- *2 tablespoons* ground cinnamon
- *½ cup (115 g)* or *1 stick* of unsalted melted butter plus some more unsalted butter for the pans

*O*H!OH!OH! Santa came last night and left presents for all! But before we open the presents, let's whip up a batch of these wonderfully scented treats! Your house will be filled with aromas of cinnamon and sugar and by the time all the presents are unwrapped, the popovers will be ready for all to enjoy. Certainly, this can become a family breakfast tradition, as they are quick and easy to make. This recipe was kindly passed to me by a lady I knew many years ago, when I used to visit the British region of Yorkshire. I thought I had lost it, but I found it on a piece of paper hidden between two pages of a book. What a sweet surprise!

Note: For this recipe, special popover pans are suggested, but you can use either babà molds or even better, muffin tins instead.

Method

Preheat the oven to 425°F (220°C) and place a popover pan in the oven.

In a large bowl, whisk together the milk, eggs, and melted butter.

In another large bowl, whisk together the flour, baking powder, and salt. Add to the milk mixture and whisk until fully incorporated. Let rest for 30 minutes at room temperature.

Carefully remove the popover pan from the oven and lower the oven temperature to 350°F (180°C).

Spray each cavity with cooking spray and drop a pad of butter in each. Using a ladle, fill each cavity with batter almost to the top. Bake for 15 minutes, then lower the oven temperature to 325°F (160°C) and bake for 20 minutes or until golden and fully risen. Remove from the oven and pierce each popover with a knife to release steam. Transfer pan to a wire rack and let cool.

To finish, combine the sugar and cinnamon in a medium-sized bowl and mix well. When the popovers are cool to the touch, brush them with the melted butter and roll in the cinnamon sugar until perfectly coated. Enjoy with a nice cup of coffee or tea!

Torta Delle Rose Mantovana
ROSE CAKE FROM MANTOVA

Ingredients

6/8 servings

For the starter
- *1 ounce (25g)* fresh yeast or ¼ ounce (6.25g) active dry yeast
- *2 teaspoons* granulated sugar
- *⅓ cup* plus *1 tablespoon (90ml)* water, lukewarm
- *⅔ cups* plus *1 tablespoon (110 g)* Manitoba flour (alternatively, bread flour)

For the dough
- *4 ⅔ cups (700g)* Manitoba flour (alternatively, bread flour)
- *¾ cup* plus *1 tablespoon (160g)* granulated sugar
- *⅓ cup* plus *1 tablespoon (90g)* unsalted butter, at room temperature
- Pinch of salt
- *5 medium-sized* organic eggs
- Freshly-grated zest of *1* organic lemon
- *2 teaspoons* vanilla bean paste or pure vanilla extract
- *1 ¼ cups (300ml)* whole milk, plus more for brushing
- Confectioners' sugar, to dust over the cake

For the filling
- *1 ¼ cups (250g)* sugar
- *1 ⅛ cups (250g)* unsalted butter

*T*his is not a traditional Christmas cake, but because it's a yeast bread, I think it's worth baking during the holidays. It dates back to the year 1490 when it was created to celebrate the marriage of Isabella D'Este, to whom it was especially dedicated, and Francesco Gonzaga, Duke of Mantova.

Shaped like a pretty bouquet of roses, this delicious cake shouts, "celebration!" It is perfect for Christmas day breakfast, but truth be told, it is delicious all year round and at any time of the day. I dedicate this recipe to my dear friend, Giovanni—Giò, as called by us friends. He loves this cake and I know that he, being born in Lombardy, is always the first to want a slice! To him I say, "Yes Giò, I have added the right amount of butter, just as you like it!"

Method

Make the starter in a medium-sized bowl by breaking the fresh yeast into crumbles. Add the granulated sugar and lukewarm water and mix until combined. Add the flour and mix without stressing the dough too much, just until a dough forms. Cover the bowl with plastic wrap and let it rest for 1 ½ hours.

Make the dough in the bowl of a stand mixer fitted with the paddle attachment. Stir together the flour, sugar, butter, and salt. Add the eggs and beat for 1 minute to combine. Add the starter, lemon zest, and vanilla and beat until fully incorporated.

With the mixer on low, add the milk in a slow, steady stream and continue beating until a smooth dough forms that doesn't stick to the sides of the bowl anymore. Transfer to a large bowl, cover with plastic wrap, and let proof in a warm place for 1 ½ hours or until doubled in volume.

Make the filling in the bowl of a stand mixer fitted with the paddle attachment. Beat the sugar and butter until creamy. Let stand at room temperature.

Lightly butter and flour a 9 to 10-inch (23 to 25-cm) round baking pan.

Transfer the dough to a lightly-floured baking sheet and using a rolling pin, roll out to about ¼-inch (0.5-cm) thick, shaping the dough into a rectangle. Spread the filling all over the surface.

With the longer side facing you, lift the baking sheet and start rolling the dough to create a loose log. Cut the log crosswise into 10 equal pieces, then arrange the rolls in a vertical position (cut side down) in the prepared baking pan. Don't pack the rolls too tightly; they need space to rise properly. Let proof in a warm place for 2 hours or until doubled in volume.

Preheat the oven to 350°F (180°C).

Using a pastry brush, gently brush a little milk over the entire cake. Bake for about 40 minutes or until golden on the top. Let the cake cool completely in the pan, then sprinkle with confectioners' sugar and serve.

Panforte Di Siena

Ingredients

4 servings

- *4 ounces (100g)* whole peeled almonds
- *4 ounces (100g)* whole peeled hazelnuts
- *4 ¾ ounces (120g)* candied orange peel, cut into small pieces
- *4 ¾ ounces (120g)* candied citron or organic lemon peel, cut into small pieces
- *4 ½ ounces (100g)* candied melon
- *⅓ cup* plus *1 tablespoon (50g)* all-purpose flour
- *½ cup (50g)* unsweetened cocoa powder
- *1 tablespoon (15g)* ground cinnamon, plus more for dusting
- *⅔ cup (130g)* granulated sugar
- *5 ounces (130g)* clear liquid honey
- Confectioners' sugar and ground cinnamon, to decorate
- *1 wafer paper* (to cut a Ø 20cm round disc)

I know every country in the world that celebrates Christmas has in their culinary repertoire some kind of fruit and spice cake, and Italians are no different. In Tuscany, in the beautiful town of Siena, they've made a cake called panforte since the early Middle Ages. During this time, Siena was a strategic commercial base. Spices were brought into the country and spice cakes and other dishes became a popular luxury product in Italy. After 1400, this cake became a symbol of wealth at aristocratic courts around Italy. An alternative version of panforte, called panepato, was created to honor Queen Margherita di Savoia when she visited Siena for Palio, the annual horse race in 1879. Panforte is a must at Christmas in Tuscany, but it is available all year round.

Method

Preheat the oven to 300°F (150°C) and line a baking sheet with parchment paper. Cut the wafer paper into an 8-inch (20-cm) round and use it to line an 8-inch (20-cm) round cake pan.

Spread the almonds and hazelnuts in an even layer on the parchment-lined baking sheet and toast for about 10 minutes. Let cool completely.

In a large bowl, combine the almonds, hazelnuts, candied orange, citron, and melon, the flour, cocoa powder, and cinnamon.

In a medium-sized saucepan over low heat, combine the sugar and honey and let melt until fully combined (stirring often to prevent burning). Add to the fruit and nut mixture and stir until incorporated. Transfer to the wafer paper–lined pan and press into an even layer. Bake for about 35 minutes, or until a wooden toothpick inserted in the center comes out clean. Dust with a generous amount of confectioners' sugar and cinnamon and serve. The panforte keeps very well if wrapped in plastic wrap or stored in any container. It makes a great present to give during the holidays. It works magic with a glass of sweet wine!

Rum Cake

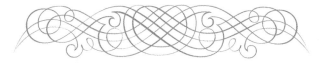

Ingredients

12 slices

For the syrup
- *1 cup (200g)* sugar
- *½ cup (115g)* or *1 stick* unsalted butter
- *⅓ cup* plus *2 tablespoons* plus *2 teaspoons (115ml)* rum
- *¼ teaspoon* salt
- *1 teaspoon* vanilla bean paste or pure vanilla extract

For the cake
- *3 ¼ cups (420g)* sifted all-purpose flour
- *½ teaspoon* salt
- *¾ cup* plus *1 tablespoon* plus *1 teaspoon (200 ml)* heavy cream, at room temperature
- *⅓ cup* plus *1 tablespoon* plus *1 teaspoon (100 ml)* rum
- *2 teaspoons* pure vanilla extract
- *3 cups (600g)* sugar
- *1 cup (230g)* or *2 sticks* unsalted butter, at room temperature
- *7* large organic eggs

*A*LERT! *This cake is seriously boozy and in the best possible way. Some people don't like alcohol in their desserts, but many do, including me. I don't like alcohol in all desserts, but when the recipe calls for it, I truly don't mind. In some cakes the alcohol evaporates during baking, leaving just a wonderful and subtle aroma. However, in this case, rum is added to the batter as well as after baking, so there's no escape. It's perfect for a New Year's Eve party. For those lucky to have a fireplace in their house, I recommend grabbing a chair or soft pillows and enjoying this dense cake while sitting by the fire. And be sure to pour yourself a glass of whatever you like, be it more booze or simply a cup of tea. I know a scenario like this would make me incredibly happy. If you don't have a fireplace, don't despair! This cake will make you happy and warm just the same!*

Note: The traditional recipe calls for vanilla pudding mix, but I skip that. As I've often stated, I always advocate for real ingredients and would prefer not to add a manufactured powder mix to my cakes. So, here is my take on the traditional version, made with real ingredients. It's your job to choose the absolute best you can find.

Method

Make the syrup in a medium-sized saucepan. Combine the sugar, butter, rum, salt, and ¼ cup (60 ml) of water. Bring to a boil and continue boiling for about 8 minutes or until thick. Remove from the heat, then stir in the vanilla and let cool at room temperature.

Butter and flour your favorite 10-inch (25-cm) bundt pan.

Make the cake batter in a large bowl. Whisk together the sifted flour and salt. In a medium-sized bowl, whisk together the cream, rum, and vanilla.

In the bowl of a stand mixer fitted with the paddle attachment, beat the sugar and butter until very pale and fluffy. Add the eggs 1 at a time, and beat until fully incorporated. Add the flour mixture, followed by the cream mixture, in 3 additions, starting and ending with the flour. Pour into the prepared pan and bake for about 50 minutes, or until a wooden toothpick inserted in the center of the cake comes out clean. Leaving the cake in the pan, poke holes all over the surface and pour some of the syrup over the top. Repeat with more syrup, reserving some for serving. (If you want extra syrup for serving, make a double batch.) Remove from the pan, cut into slices, and serve with vanilla ice cream.

Babà

*B*abà! The King of Naples! Well known everywhere in the country and appreciated all over the world. It is a brioche-like preparation, drenched in a boozy syrup made with dark rum and all sorts of winter spices. It can be baked in single molds, in round baking pans, or as I did this time, it can baked in the traditional 11-inch fluted Babà mold. You can easily find one on the internet, so don't be worried. The making of this recipe requires some time and some baking skills, but if you follow the recipe closely, you won't fail. Just, be patient. This is a great recipe, which will make you a Master home baker!

Ingredients

10 servings

For the dough
- *2 tablespoons* water, at room temperature
- *1 ounce (25g)* fresh yeast, cut into small pieces
- *3 ¾ cups (500g)* bread flour
- *Scant ⅓ cup (60g)* sugar
- 8 large organic eggs, at room temperature and lightly whisked
- *½ cup plus 3 tablespoons (160g)* unsalted butter, at room temperature and cut into cubes

For the syrup (bagna)
- *1* organic orange
- *1* medium-sized organic lemon
- *2 ¼ cups (450g)* sugar
- *1 ½ teaspoons* vanilla bean paste or pure vanilla extract
- *1* cinnamon stick
- *¾ cup plus 2 tablespoons (220ml)* dark rum, preferably 70° proof
- Pastry cream or whipped cream, for serving (optional)

Method

Pour the room temperature water into a small bowl, sprinkle with the fresh yeast, and stir until completely dissolved. Add ¼ cup plus 2 tablespoons (50g) of the bread flour and mix by hand until a dough is formed. Shape the dough into a ball, then place it in a slightly floured large bowl covered with plastic wrap. Let rest in a warm place for 1 hour. This is called the "biga."

In the bowl of a stand mixer fitted with the paddle attachment, combine the sugar and the remaining 3 ¼ cups plus 2 tablespoons (450g) of bread flour and mix on low until combined. Gradually add the eggs, beating well after each one, and mixing until fully incorporated. Add the biga and beat on medium for 15 minutes. The dough will be sticky. Switch to the

bread hook attachment. With the mixer on medium, gradually add the butter in small portions, kneading until the butter is completely incorporated before adding more. Continue kneading for another 15 to 20 minutes or until the dough looks very elastic and shiny. Using a rubber spatula, clean the sides of the bowl, then gather the dough in the center of the bowl and cover with plastic wrap, making sure it doesn't touch the dough and there is enough space for the dough to rise properly. Let the dough rest in a warm place for 1 ½ hours or until tripled in volume.

Preheat the oven to 350°F (180°C). Use a pastry brush to brush the inside of a Babà mold with butter. Gently place the dough inside the mold, making sure not to deflate it, and let rest for 1 ½ hours, or until doubled in size. Bake for 25 to 30 minutes. Let cool completely, then remove from the mold.

For the syrup, peel the orange and lemon and place the peels in a medium-sized saucepan; reserve the fruit for another use. Add the sugar, vanilla, cinnamon stick, and 4 cups (1 liter) of water, then bring to a boil over medium heat. Add the rum and cook for 5 minutes, then remove from the heat and let cool until room temperature.

Place the Babà in a bowl or deep cake pan, pour the syrup over it, and let it sit until the syrup is completely absorbed. Transfer the Babà to a serving plate. Decorate with whipped cream or pastry cream if desired, and serve.

Veneziana

Ingredients

8 servings

For the dough
- *1 ounce (25g fresh or 7g active dry)* yeast
- *¾ cup plus 1 tablespoon plus 1 teaspoon (200ml)* whole milk, lukewarm
- *2* large organic eggs, at room temperature, plus *1* large organic egg yolk for glazing
- *7 tablespoons (90g)* granulated sugar
- Seeds scraped from *1* vanilla bean pod
- Freshly-grated zest of *½* organic orange
- *½ cup plus 1 teaspoon (120g)* unsalted butter, melted and cooled
- *4 cups (500g)* Manitoba flour (alternatively, bread flour), sifted
- *½ teaspoon* salt
- Pearl sugar, to decorate
- Confectioners' sugar, to decorate

For the pastry cream
- *2* large egg yolks
- *Scant ⅓ cup (60g)* granulated sugar
- *3 tablespoons (24g)* organic cornstarch
- Pinch of salt
- *2 cups plus 1 tablespoon plus 1 teaspoon (500ml)* whole milk
- *1 teaspoon* vanilla bean paste or pure vanilla extract or seeds scraped from *1* vanilla bean pod

*D*o not be fooled by the name of this delicious brioche-like delicacy. "Veneziana" is not a recipe from Venice. Its origins date back to the fifteenth century in the Italian Region of Lombardia, where it used to be prepared for weddings and Christmas festivities. Now every café in Italy, especially in the north, displays freshly baked "veneziane" every morning for breakfast. This version has been adapted for home bakers, so you can enjoy "veneziana" anytime you want. I bake this recipe in a single pan, but you can divide the dough into balls and follow the same exact method to make individual portions.

Note: There may be leftover pastry cream, which can be reserved and used for other desserts.

Method

Make the dough in a medium-sized bowl. Crumble the fresh yeast into the lukewarm milk and stir until fully dissolved.

In the bowl of a stand mixer fitted with the paddle attachment, beat the 2 large eggs and the granulated sugar until pale. Add the vanilla and orange zest, followed by the melted butter, and beat until incorporated. Add the yeast mixture and beat until fully combined. Add the flour and beat just enough to incorporate. Add the salt, switch to the bread hook attachment and knead for at least 6 minutes, or until a smooth dough forms and doesn't stick to the sides of the bowl anymore. Gather the dough into a smooth ball, place it in a large bowl, cover with plastic wrap, and let proof in a warm place for 1 ½ hours or until doubled in size.

Make the pastry cream in a medium-sized bowl. Combine the egg yolks, granulated sugar, cornstarch, and salt and whisk until pale.

In a medium-sized saucepan over medium heat, bring the milk and vanilla to a gentle boil. Add a small amount to the egg yolk mixture and quickly stir to temper the eggs. Pour the tempered egg yolk mixture into the saucepan, whisking constantly until thick. Transfer to a bowl, cover with plastic wrap, and let cool.

Transfer the proofed dough to a lightly-floured work surface and knead a little without stressing it too much.

Lightly butter and flour a 9 ½-inch (24 cm) round baking pan, place the dough inside, and let proof in a warm place (like a closed oven) for about 1 ½ hours or until doubled in size.

Preheat the oven to 350°F (180°C).

Brush the dough with the remaining egg yolk. Using a sharp knife, score the center with an "X" then carefully open the cut without going so far that the dough deflates. Fill a piping bag with the pastry cream and pipe some in the center of the dough, letting it spread over the top a little, but keeping it in the center as much as possible. Sprinkle the entire surface with pearl sugar and bake for about 45 minutes or until golden on the top. Let cool, then sprinkle all over with confectioners' sugar and proudly serve!

Gubana Friulana

GUBANA FROM FRIULI

Ingredients

6/8 servings

For the filling
- *¾ cup (100g)* raisins
- *2 tablespoons (30ml)* grappa, plus more as needed
- *⅓ cup (70g)* sugar
- *6 ounces (150g)* walnuts
- *1 ½ ounces (40g)* pine nuts
- *2 tablespoons (30g)* unsalted butter, plus some extra butter curls
- *3 ¼ ounces (80g)* amaretti cookies
- Freshly-grated zest of *1* organic lemon
- 1 teaspoon vanilla bean paste or pure vanilla extract
- *1 teaspoon* ground cinnamon
- Pinch of salt

For the dough (it is not a cake, but a yeasted bread)
- *1* large organic egg white
- *3 tablespoons* plus *1 teaspoon (50ml)* whole milk, lukewarm
- *½ ounce (12g)* fresh yeast
- *1 ¾ cups* plus *3 tablespoons (250g)* all-purpose flour
- *Scant ⅓ cup (60g)* sugar
- *1* large organic egg plus *1* large organic egg yolk
- Pinch of salt
- *¼ cup* plus *2 teaspoons (70g)* unsalted butter, cut into small cubes and softened
- *1 ½ ounces (40g)* clear liquid honey

*M*y family, on my father's side, comes from the beautiful region of Friuli in northern Italy and, more specifically, from The Natisone Valley. Therefore, it's fitting for me to present you with one of the local cakes I used to eat there as a child at Christmas. I haven't managed to get my hands on the original recipe—this cake dates back to 1409—but this version is the closest I could come up with after many years of tasting. It is tender, boozy, sweet, aromatic, and full of interesting textures. In Friuli, it is made during the holidays and served with a glass of grappa, which is another specialty of the region. Though it's not super easy to make, thanks to the complexity of its flavors and textures, this cake provides great satisfaction when presented at the table. It's not for the faint of heart, given that the process of preparation is very traditional and exacting. Because the recipe is so dear to me, and dear to the people of Friuli, the recipe leaves no space for improvisation.

Note: The filling for this cake needs to be made a day in advance.

Method

Make the filling in a small bowl. Soak the raisins in the grappa for 1 hour.

In a medium-sized saucepan over low heat, cook the sugar until completely melted and almost caramelized. Add about a handful of the walnuts and quickly toss them in the caramel. Invert the caramelized walnuts onto a sheet of parchment paper and let cool at room temperature.

In a small saucepan, stir together the pine nuts and butter and cook until the butter completely coats the pine nuts. Let cool at room temperature.

On a cutting board, combine the caramelized walnuts, the plain walnuts, the pine nuts, and the raisins with the grappa they soaked in, along with the amaretti cookies, lemon zest, vanilla, cinnamon, and salt and chop into very small pieces. If the mixture is too dry, add additional grappa as needed. Place all ingredients in a medium-sized bowl, cover with plastic wrap and leave to rest at room temperature overnight.

The next day make the dough. In a small bowl, combine the lukewarm milk and yeast and stir until the yeast is completely dissolved.

In the bowl of a stand mixer fitted with the paddle attachment, combine the flour, the milk and yeast mixture, the egg and egg yolk, honey, sugar and salt. Add the butter, piece by piece, and mix until a dough starts to form. Switch to the dough hook attachment and knead on high for about 15 minutes, or until a ball of dough forms and doesn't stick to the sides of the bowl anymore. Cover the bowl with plastic wrap and let rest in a warm place for 1 ½ hours or until doubled in volume.

Preheat the oven to 350°F (180°C). Butter and flour an 8-inch (20-cm) round cake pan.

On a lightly-floured work surface, use a rolling pin to roll out the dough into a rectangle. Spread the filling over the entire surface and sprinkle with some butter curls. Using your hands, roll the dough around the filling into a long sausage shape, sealing the ends. Roll the dough into a snail shape and arrange in the prepared cake pan. Cover the pan with plastic wrap and let proof at room temperature for 1 ½ hours. Brush the entire surface of the cake with the egg white and bake for about 50 minutes, or until fully baked and golden on the top. Let cool completely before serving.

Mallorca Buns

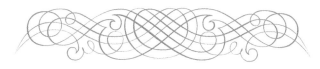

Ingredients

12 buns

- *1 ¼ cups* plus *3 tablespoons (350ml)* water, at room temperature
- *½ cup (120ml)* whole milk, lukewarm
- *1 ¼ tablespoons (7g)* active dry yeast
- *8 large* organic egg yolks
- *¾ cup (150g)* granulated sugar
- *1 ½ cups (340g)* unsalted butter, melted and cooled to room temperature, plus more for brushing
- *6 cups* plus *2 tablespoons (800g)* bread flour
- *1 teaspoon* salt
- Confectioners' sugar, to decorate
- Extra flour to dust the work surface

*T*hese buns will be the rival of French toast. Whether for a holiday or special occasion, breakfast and brunch will never be the same! In other words, these are special. They can be cut open and filled with jam, chocolate spread, pastry cream, or any cream you like. They are also amazing filled with savory ingredients, which makes them good dinner rolls, too—just avoid the icing sugar at the end, of course. Originally made in Spain, Mallorca buns are now a Puerto Rican tradition. And if you, dear reader, live in a country where it's cold at Christmas, these buns will bring sunshine to your day!

Method

In a medium-sized bowl, combine the room temperature water and the milk. Sprinkle with the yeast and set aside.

In the bowl of a stand mixer fitted with the whisk attachment, combine the egg yolks, salt, sugar, and melted butter and whip until incorporated. Add the yeast mixture and whip on medium speed until combined. Switch to the dough hook

attachment and with the mixer on low, add the flour in intervals. Once the flour has been incorporated, turn the mixer to high and continue beating for about 15 minutes. After this time the dough will be shiny and still very sticky, but don't worry, it will come together. Transfer the dough to a well-floured work surface and knead until smooth. Gather the dough into a ball, place inside a large bowl, cover with plastic wrap, and let proof for 2 hours in a warm place or until doubled in volume.

Line 2 baking sheets with parchment paper.

Divide the dough into 12 equal-sized balls of about 174g. Roll each ball into a rope, then curve each rope into a not-too-tight coil. Arrange the buns on the parchment-lined baking sheet, cover with a dishcloth, and let proof at room temperature for 1 hour or until doubled in size.

Preheat the oven to 350°F (180°C).

Brush the buns with melted butter, then bake for about 20 minutes or until lightly golden. Let cool, then sprinkle with confectioners' sugar and serve.

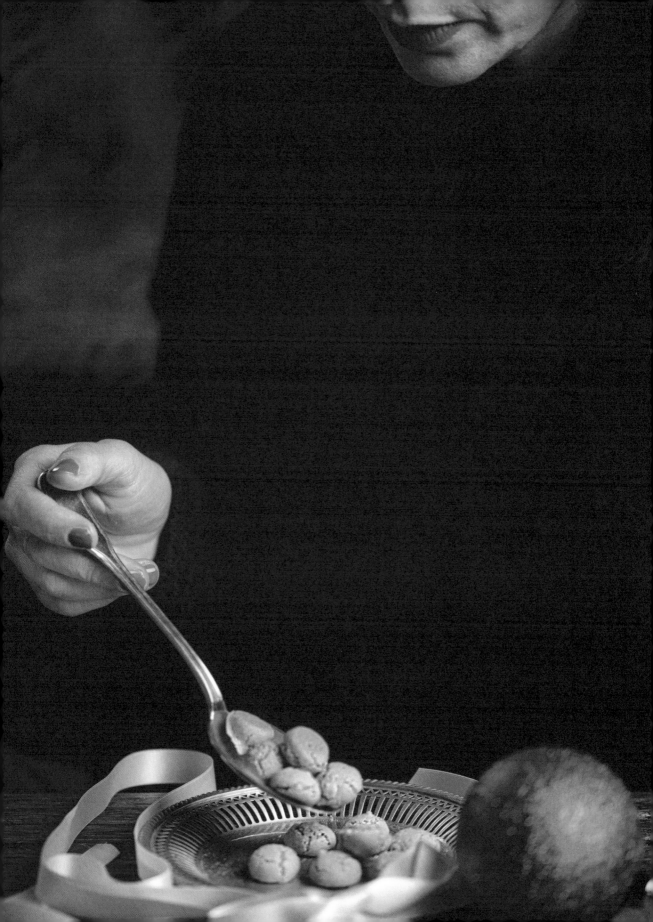

Milk Pan Del Molise

Ingredients

About 8/10 slices

For the cake
- *1 ¼ cups (160g)* all-purpose flour, sifted
- *1 cup* plus *1 tablespoon (140g)* potato starch
- *1 ½ teaspoons* baking powder
- *6* large organic eggs, separated
- *1 ¼ cups (250g)* sugar
- *1 ⅓ cups (300g)* unsalted butter, melted and cooled to room temperature
- *½ cup (125ml)* cream milk liqueur or Baileys
- *1 teaspoon* vanilla bean paste or pure vanilla extract
- Pinch of salt

For the glaze
- *8 ounces (200 g)* good quality white chocolate, melted
- *2 tablespoons* vegetable oil
- *2 tablespoons* hazelnut paste*

* Check organic shops for pure hazelnut paste, but if you can't find it, use a good quality hazelnut spread.

*T*his dessert comes from southern Italy, and more precisely, from the region of Molise. The recipe has garnered a lot of controversy over the years. Apparently, the only traditional ingredient in the recipe is a liqueur called "liquore crema milk," created around the year 1840, which is the cake's namesake. For many years, this liqueur could pretty much only be found in Molise, but you can now order it online! If you can't get your hands on it, you can substitute with Baileys, but it won't be the same. I don't intend to mislead you, my dear reader, or to spoil the original recipe, but I know how daunting it can be to find ingredients at times. It would be a pity not to make this cake only because you can't find the specific liqueur. It is delicious, and so like poets often do, I exercise my "baker's license" to change a single ingredient. Milk Pan Del Molise is typically baked in a dome-shaped pan, but a bundt pan works, too. It looks great when served at the Christmas table and because it is such an unknown recipe, I knew I had to share it with all of you. I hope you bake it soon! You will see—it won't last long.

Method

Preheat the oven to 350°F (175°C). Butter and flour a dome-shaped cake pan with an 8-inch base.

In a large bowl, sift together the flour, potato starch, and baking powder.

In the bowl of a stand mixer fitted with the paddle attachment or using a hand-held mixer, beat the egg yolks and sugar until very pale. Add the melted and cooled butter and the liqueur in a steady stream and beat until incorporated. Add the flour mixture and beat until combined. Transfer to a large bowl.

Clean the bowl of the stand mixer and use the whisk attachment to whip the egg whites and salt until stiff peaks form, then gently fold them into the batter. Pour into the prepared pan and bake for 40 to 45 minutes, or until a wooden toothpick inserted in the center of the cake comes out clean. Let cool completely in the pan, then invert onto a wire rack.

Make the glaze in a bain-marie or a metal bowl set over a pan of simmering water. Melt the white chocolate, stirring occasionally. Alternatively, you can melt the chocolate in the microwave in 5 second intervals, but be careful, as white chocolate burns quickly. Add the vegetable oil and hazelnut paste and stir until completely combined. Pour the glaze over the cooled cake and let set at room temperature. Serve as is or decorate using your creativity.

Panettone

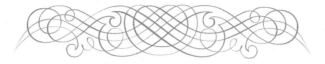

Ingredients

About 6/8 servings

For the aroma mix
- *1 ¼ ounces (30g)* clear liquid honey, like acacia honey
- Seeds scraped from *2* vanilla beans
- Freshly-grated zest of *1* large organic orange
- Freshly-grated zest of *1* organic lemon

For the "biga"
- *⅝ cup (80g)* Manitoba flour (alternatively, bread flour)
- *3 ¼ ounces (80g)* water, lukewarm (about 80°F / 27°C)
- *½ ounce (12g)* fresh yeast
- *1 teaspoon* sugar

For the dough
- *10 ounces (250g)* raisins or chocolate chips
- *1 ⅔ cups (200g)* Manitoba flour (alternatively, bread flour)
- *1 cup plus 1 tablespoon (160g)* flour type 0
- *⅔ cup (150ml)* water, lukewarm (about 80°F / 27°C)
- *½ cup (100g)* sugar
- *4 large organic egg yolks*
- *1 teaspoon (5g)* salt
- *⅓ cup plus 2 tablespoons (100g)* unsalted butter, at room temperature, plus *1 to 1 ½ tablespoons (15 to 20g)* unsalted butter, melted
- *10 ounces (250g)* candied orange peel, cut into small chunks

Bell chimes Hear!! Hear!! I present you the king of Christmas cakes!! His majesty, The Panettone! I bow in the presence of this majestic cake—one of the most difficult, but also one of the most rewarding. This is a simpler take on the classic recipe. I must confess that even I don't follow the real technique, and the reason is that Panettone has changed over the years to meet the ever-growing demand. And thus, industrial (and even, unfortunately, some artisan bakeries) use special chemicals, preservatives, and additives to prolong the life of Panettone and to achieve the pillow-like texture we all love. Without getting into the many steps and the proofing time required, the traditional method produced a different and more dense cake because it was made by hand and without chemicals. My wish is to stick to the real deal while still enjoying a successful Panettone at Christmas. So, if you are looking for something similar to the Panettone you buy in shops, then feel free to buy one, but don't give up on trying to make your own. I prescribe a good dose of patience, a lot of calming music in the background, and some serious self-confidence. I did it. You can do it, too.

Method

Make the aroma mix in a small bowl by stirring together the honey, vanilla, and orange and lemon zest. Cover with plastic wrap and let stand for at least 1 hour.

Make the "biga" in a small bowl by combining the flour, lukewarm water, yeast, and sugar and stir until the yeast is completely dissolved. Cover with plastic wrap and let stand at room temperature for about 1 hour or until doubled in volume.

If using raisins, place them in a medium-sized bowl with water and let stand for at least 1 hour so they have enough time to rehydrate.

Butter a large bowl. In the bowl of a stand mixer fitted with the dough hook attachment, combine the flour, the lukewarm water, sugar, egg yolks, and salt. Knead on medium-low for 10 to 15 minutes. Add the "biga" and knead for 8 minutes, then add the aroma mix and knead until combined. With the mixer on medium speed, slowly add the room temperature butter in small additions, then knead for 5 minutes or until fully incorporated. Drain the raisins and pat them dry, then add to the dough and mix until the raisins are fully

→

incorporated and the dough stops sticking to the sides of the bowl.

Butter a clean work surface. Gently allow the dough to fall from the bowl onto the counter without pressing or flattening it. Slowly and gently lift up the dough with yours hands as if puffing up a pillow—the dough should look like a soft and fluffy pillow. Rotate the dough about 10 times, being very careful not to stress the dough, which is key for a successful resting time and creating the perfect texture. Place the dough in the large buttered bowl, cov-

er with plastic wrap, making sure no air penetrates inside the bowl. Place in the oven and let rest for about 12 hours.

Remove the dough from the bowl and set it on a lightly-floured work surface. Being very gentle, fold the dough into 3 parts, thereby trapping the air inside the dough. Shape the dough into a ball to guarantee a round shape during baking and then gently place it in a 40-ounce (1 kg) tall paper Panettone mold. Cover with plastic wrap, return to the oven, and let rest for about 1 hour or until it doubled in volume.

Set a rack in the lower third of the oven and preheat the oven to 350°F (180°C).

At this point, the dough has risen into a dome. Remove the plastic wrap from the Panettone and with a very sharp knife, make 2 shallow, crosswise cuts. Using your hands, lift the 4 corners, as if you were to peel the skin off, and pull the extremities towards the outside of the Panettone. Place a small (approximately 5g) piece of butter in the center. Brush the Panettone with the melted butter and bake on the lower rack of the oven for 45 to 50 minutes, or until a wooden toothpick inserted in the center comes out clean. Remove from the oven and insert two long metal Panettone skewers through the paper mold. Flip the Panettone and place it upside down inside a large, deep pan so the ends of the skewers are set over the edge of the pan, and the Panettone hangs inside the pan. Let cool completely, then invert the cake, cut slices and enjoy with a glass of sweet wine at the end of your Christmas lunch or dinner!

Ghirlanda di Natale

CHRISTMAS WREATH

Ingredients

6/8 servings

- *2 ¼ teaspoons (7g)* or *1 pack* of active dry yeast
- *5 tablespoons (80ml)* lukewarm water
- *½ cup (120ml)* lukewarm milk
- *¼ cup (60g)* melted butter, cooled to room temperature
- *2* large organic egg yolks
- *4 cups (500g)* all-purpose flour
- *¼ cup (50g)* sugar
- *½ teaspoon (3g)* salt
- Confectioners' sugar, for dusting
- *1* organic beaten egg, for brushing

For the filling

- *⅔ cup (150g)* butter, at room temperature
- *¼ cup (50g)* sugar
- *1 ½ teaspoons* ground cinnamon (or more if you like it)
- Grated zest of *1* large organic lemon
- *1 teaspoon* vanilla paste or the scraped seeds of *1* vanilla pod
- *1 cup (100g)* dried cranberries

*L*ike many of my recipes, this one is a good base to experiment with different flavor combinations. Edible Christmas wreaths are all over the place lately, on the internet or in other baking books. They are pretty, fun to make and, honestly, quite simple. For those who are not familiar with yeast doughs, or for those out there who are scared to even try to cook with yeast dough, this is for you. Follow the steps closely and you will not fail. This recipe will win your heart and boost your confidence, and I am pretty sure you will want to make it again and again! You can play with different ingredients for an Easter version to bring to a picnic, for example. Why not? But for now, let's stick to Christmas and make what will proclaim you "Official Holiday Baker!"

Method

Combine the yeast and water in a small bowl and stir until the yeast is fully dissolved. Set aside. Combine the flour, sugar, and salt in a large bowl and set aside.

In a bowl of a stand mixer fitted with the dough hook, combine the milk, cooled melted butter, and the egg yolks. With the machine on low, beat the ingredients until completely mixed in. Add the yeast and water mixture and beat until fully incorporated. Add the flour, sugar, and salt. On low speed, beat for about 4 minutes, or until the dough looks smooth and stops sticking to the sides of the bowl.

Stop the machine, invert the dough on your work table and gather it into a ball. Place the dough in a lightly-floured large bowl, cover with plastic wrap, and allow to proof in a warm place for 1 hour. In the meantime, prepare the filling by combining all of the ingredients in a medium-sized bowl and stirring them all together using a spatula or spoon until creamy, smooth and fully combined. Set aside.

Line a baking tray with a sheet of parchment paper and set aside. Remove the dough from the bowl and roll it on a lightly-floured surface into a 22 x 12-inch (56 x 30-cm) rectangle. Spread the butter filling evenly all over the surface of the rolled dough, all the way to the edges.

With the long side facing you, roll up the dough tightly to form a long sausage shape. Turn the roll so the seam side faces up. Take a sharp knife and cut the log lengthwise along the seam.

Join the top edges together, gently lift the log and transfer it on to the baking tray. Brush the joined top with the beaten egg to seal. Weave both halves. Brush one woven end with more egg wash and form into a wreath, pinching the egg wash end and tucking the other underneath. Cover loosely with plastic wrap and allow to proof for another hour in a warm place.

Preheat the oven to 180°C / 325°F. Bake for about 40 minutes or until golden in color. Cool and dust with icing sugar right before serving.

Mini Pandori

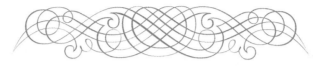

I thought a lot about whether or not to add this recipe to my Christmas book. Pandoro, like panettone, is probably one of the most time-consuming and complicated recipes ever created. The texture is achieved through hours of proofing and the final result is different from manufactured products. But Christmas to us Italians isn't Christmas without it, and so, I opted for an "easier" version. Of course, you can buy a large pandoro in any good shop these days, but I think there is a special pleasure to be found in making things yourself. Hence, my recipe for mini pandori. You will need special mini pandori silicone molds or individual aluminum molds, which are easily found online. You can serve pandori as individual cakes, perhaps paired with some brandy sauce, or you can give them to your kids to bring to school to enjoy during a break. Finally, and this is what I prefer, you can warm them slightly, slice them in half, and drop a dollop of chocolate spread in the middle for a super indulgent breakfast!

Ingredients

Makes 12 small pandorini

For the emulsion
- Freshly-grated zest of *1* large organic orange
- *1 tablespoon* clear honey
- *1 tablespoon* vanilla bean paste or seeds scraped from *1* vanilla bean
- *1 tablespoon* rum

For the pandorini
- *2 cups* plus *1 tablespoon (270g)* Manitoba flour (alternatively, bread flour)
- *⅓ cup (75ml)* water, lukewarm
- *½ teaspoon (3g)* active dry yeast (or *¼ ounce / 6.25g* fresh yeast)
- *1 teaspoon* clear liquid honey
- *1 ¾ ounces (45g)* good quality white chocolate
- *¼ cup* plus *2 tablespoons (80g)* granulated sugar
- *3 tablespoons* plus *1 teaspoon (50ml)* whole milk, at room temperature
- *1* large organic egg
- *⅓ cup* plus *1 teapoon (80g)* unsalted butter, at room tempearture and cut into small
- *½ teaspoon* salt
- Confectioners' sugar, to decorate

Method

One day before serving, make the emulsion.

In a medium-sized bowl, combine the orange zest, honey, vanilla, and rum. Cover with plastic wrap and let rest at room temperature for at least 1 day.

Make the starter in the bowl of a stand mixer fitted with the paddle attachment. Combine ½ cup plus 1 tablespoon (75g) of flour, the lukewarm water, the yeast, and the honey. Beat until the ingredients are combined and a soft dough forms. Cover with plastic wrap and let rest at about 80°F (27°C) for 2 hours or until doubled in volume.

In a bain-marie or metal bowl set over a pan of simmering water, melt the white chocolate while stirring occasionally, then let cool at room temperature.

After the first proofing, add the remaining 1 ½ cups (195g) of flour, salt, sugar, and milk and mix on low until fully incorporated. Add the emulsion, followed by the egg, and beat until the dough sticks to the paddle attachment without leaving any traces around the bowl. Add the melted and cooled chocolate and mix on low, occasionally scraping down the sides of the bowl. Don't overwork (stress or press) the dough.

Switch to the dough hook attachment and with the mixer on low, gradually add the butter, a little at a time, and knead until fully incorporated. Knead for about 25 minutes, occasionally checking the elasticity by placing the dough on a work surface and stretching to see if it breaks or not. Transfer the dough to a work surface and knead it by hand, folding the sides in 4 parts and being careful not to pop any of the air pockets (as they are essential to good results).

Cut the dough into balls, roughly 2 ounces (50g) each, then place them smooth side down inside 12 silicone pandorini molds. Let proof in a warm place for 4 hours or until doubled in volume. Bake for 20 to 25 minutes at 356°F (180°C) or until golden (but not too much). If the pandorini color too fast, cover them with aluminum foil. Let cool in the molds for about 5 minutes, then release onto the counter and let cool completely. Dust with confectioners' sugar. Pandorini can be stored in an airtight container at room temperature for up to 2 days.

Christmas Buns

*When you want to show off your bak-
ing skills, these buns should be your
go-to recipe. Add raisins for a Christmas
morning delight, or slice them in half and
fill them with jam for an afternoon tea delicacy. They are a dinner party must, especially if paired with ice cream, and an after dinner sin, if you add chocolate chips!*

Ingredients

About 16 buns

- *1 ounce (25g)* fresh yeast
- *1 teaspoon* granulated sugar
- *¼ cup* plus *2 tablespoons (90g)* granulated sugar
- *1 cup* plus *2 teaspoons (250ml)* whole milk, lukewarm
- *4 cups* plus *2 tablespoons (500g)* all-purpose flour
- *1 teaspoon* salt
- *1 large organic* egg
- *⅓ cup (75g)* unsalted butter, softened and cut into small chunks
- *½ cup (70g)* raisins or chocolate chips (optional)

For the egg wash
- *1 large egg* yolk
- *2 tablespoons* whole milk

Method

Crumble the yeast into a small bowl. Add
1 teaspoon of the granulated sugar and 2
tablespoons of the lukewarm milk and let
stand at room temperature for 15 minutes.

In the bowl of a stand mixer fitted with
the paddle attachment, combine the
flour, salt, egg, the remaining 90g granulated sugar, the remaining 220ml lukewarm milk, and the yeast mixture. Beat
on medium-low until fully combined,
then switch to the bread hook attachment. With the mixer on medium speed,
gradually add the softened butter, piece
by piece. Knead the dough for about 15
minutes or until it stops sticking to the
sides of the bowl.

Transfer the dough to a clean work surface and knead by hand for 15 to 20 minutes, or until smooth. If the dough is too
sticky, gradually knead in a little more
flour. If using raisins or chocolate chips,
add them now and knead until incorporated. Continue kneading until the dough
is smooth, then transfer to a large bowl.
Cover with plastic wrap and let rise at
room temperature for about 1 ½ hours or
until doubled in size. Gently punch down
the dough to release any air bubbles,
then cover with plastic wrap again and
let proof in the refrigerator for at least 3
hours and preferably overnight.

On a clean work surface, knead the
dough into a sausage-shaped roll and
cut into pieces roughly 2 ½ ounces (65g)
each. Shape the pieces into balls.

Preheat the oven to 350°F (180°C) and
line a baking sheet with parchment paper or a silicone baking mat.

Make the egg wash in a small bowl by
whisking together the egg yolk and milk.
Use a pastry brush to brush a small
amount on each bun.

Arrange the buns about 1 ½ inches (4 cm)
apart on the parchment-lined baking sheet.
Brush another layer of egg wash on each
bun, then bake for 15 to 20 minutes or until golden. Let cool completely.

Index

© Prestel Verlag, Munich · London · New York 2020
A member of Verlagsgruppe Random House GmbH
Neumarkter Strasse 28 · 81673 Munich

© Text: Melissa Forti, 2020
© Photographs: Danny Bernardini, 2020

A CIP catalogue record for this book is available from the British Library.

Creative producer: Massimo Zannoni
Design and layout: Isabella Mancioli
Flower arrangements and props: Irene Ratti
Costumes consultant: Carlotta Cozzani

Editorial direction: Claudia Stäuble
Translation (Foreword Tim Raue): John Sykes
Copyediting: Lauren Salkeld, Meredith Hays
Production management: Friederike Schirge
Separations: Reproline Mediateam
Printing and binding: DZS Grafik, d.o.o., Ljubljana
Paper: Tauro Offset

Verlagsgruppe Random House FSC® N001967

Printed in Slovenia

ISBN 978-3-7913-8637-9

www.prestel.com

Thank you

This book has been conceived in a very difficult moment in history as well
as in my life, but nonetheless it is a work of love and joy.
I couldn't have made it without the help of very talented people.
Thank you to Prestel Verlag for believing in me once more. It means the world
to me. Thank you for ever and ever to Massimo Zannoni for the impeccable
work and for making my vision come true. Danny Bernardini for making sure
my recipes look stunning on camera! These two people are pure genius and talent.
We argue, but we manage to make miracles together!
Thank you to "La Verde Milonga," aka Irene, for the amazing flower
and plant arrangements! You talented woman! Thank you "Many me" boutique,
aka, Carlotta, for your help and stunning taste! You are a fashion guru!
Thank you to my mother, who has been so patient with me throughout the
project. I am sorry I couldn't be present all the time, but you know I love you!
My amazingly gorgeous friend, Leila, who is my kindred spirit and a pure soul
of her own. I love you, sweetie!! Serena, for being my assistant as well as a great
supporter and super friend! Love you, too! Charis, Rube, and little Olivia
for being an example of the family I wish to have one day!
Francesco and Jess, to you my love. Giò and Agnese, I love you, too! Thank you
Fabri, for giving me a chance when I moved to Sarzana and for being my
friend all these years! To the entire beautiful city of Sarzana, and to the
many wonderful people who supported my work from day one. Thank you,
from the bottom of my heart. To Tim Raue and Tim Mälzer for teaching me
so much about life in this business! Doreen, my German bestie and wonderful
human being, love you loads! Chef Micky and little Neele! Thank you for all
the laughter you have shared with me and for your help during difficult times.
Martin, a true gentleman and friend! Thank you! Laura, thank you
for helping at the shop when I couldn't be there! You are precious.
Thank you, Isabella Mancioli! My little Nina and Bianca, this book is for you, too!
And last, but definitely not least, to the most incredible person in my life, Diego.
You are my best friend, soul mate, and partner in crime. We are growing
together and loving each other in a way I have never known before.
You are my person.
Thank you for being the most surprising and yet precious gift of all! I love you.

Merry Christmas!
With love,
Melissa